On Communalism and Globalization

On Communalism and Globalization

Offensives of the Far Right

SECOND EDITION
WITH A NEW INTRODUCTION

Aijaz Ahmad

Three Essays
COLLECTIVE

Second Edition 2004
Reprinted May 2016, 2023, 2025

ISBN 978-81-88789-14-6

Three Essays
COLLECTIVE

B-957 Palam Vihar, Gurugram 122 017, India
Phone: +91 98681 26587, +91 98683 44843
threeessays@gmail.com www.threeessays.com
Printed at Replika Press Pvt. Ltd., India

For
Shadab

in Memoriam

Contents

Introduction to the Second Edition

This collection of essays was first sent to press in June 2002, in a moment of foreboding, in the aftermath of the Gujarat pogrom. Now, eighteen months later, this introduction to a second printing is being drafted in December 2003, in a terrifying interregnum between four state assembly elections three of which the BJP has swept, and the Lok Sabha elections which the BJP-led central government of the National Democratic Alliance (NDA) is trying to hold as quickly as possible.

The Gujarat pogrom was itself followed by a resounding electoral victory for the BJP in the assembly elections in that state, with Narendra Modi, the former RSS pracharak and chief architect of that pogrom, in full command; in neighbouring Rajasthan BJP had at that time gone on to win three successive by-elections, as an indication of worse things yet to come. The introduction I wrote for this book at that time ended with some comments on the election of Mr. Kalam, a nuclear hawk and a BJP nominee, to the Presidency of the Republic. That was soon followed by the rise of Bhairon Singh Shekhawat, a former BJP chief minister of Rajasthan, to the Vice Presidency of the country, a heartbeat away from the Presidency that Mr. Kalam currently holds. As of now, all the leading positions in the Republic – Prime Minister, President, Vice President, Speaker of the Lok Sabha – are held by veterans and nominees of Hindutva.

Before the pogrom began, BJP had suffered a series of setbacks in local elections and by-elections. Then, in December 2002, some nine months after that pogrom and spearheading a culture of cruelty and a politics of hate, Modi stomped to electoral victory with 126 seats out of 181, improving the previous tally of 117. The Congress trailed by 10 percentage points in the popular vote, winning barely 37 seats, down from 48. In the process, Modi demonstrated that violence, especially communal violence, pays huge electoral dividends. In deed, the violence itself had been unleashed with an eye on the electoral gains, so that only the Congress (I)'s strongholds in north and central Gujarat had been targeted. After the pogrom, BJP won 52 out of the 65 constituencies in which the pogrom had been concentrated, leading the Congress by 19 percentage points in these specific constituencies. BJP won every single seat in the vicinity of Godhra, in central Gujarat's Panchmahal, Dahod and rural Vadodara, which had witnessed the worst violence, and it won 10 out of 12 seats in Ahmedabad itself, which had been home to some of the most heinous Hindutva crimes.

In the introduction I wrote 18 months ago I had commented briefly on the ignominious role of the self-styled secular allies of the BJP in the NDA fold during and immediately after the Gujarat carnage. As the campaign for the Assembly elections picked up steam, Mayawati, the Bahujan Samaj Party's Chief Minister in UP, in power there with an alliance with the BJP, travelled to Gujarat, campaigned actively for Modi and helped him garner a substantial part of the Dalit vote. After Modi's victory, All India Anna Dravida Munnetra Kazhagam (AIADMK) general secretary and Tamil Nadu chief minister Jayalalithaa congratulated Modi on "overcoming difficulties and obstacles created by the media and a hostile Election Commission of India." As if these friends of the BJP were not enough, the Congress quickly inducted Shankarsinh Vaghela as the new Gujarat Pradesh Congress Committee president to lead the 'secular' forces against Modi – the same Modi who had worked closely with Vaghela during the mid-1980s when the latter was President of the Gujarat State unit of the BJP. The fallen hero of the BJP was now to lead the electoral battle against it, presumably to bring the Congress to power on a platform of soft Hindutva against Modi's harder, murderous one.

The debacle was there for all to see. However, the liberal media and even sections of the Left contrived to believe that Gujarat was a special case, that it could possibly not be repeated elsewhere, hoping that the nightmare would just go away and the ghost would exorcise itself. Unfortunately, Praveen Togadia, the international secretary of the Vishwa Hindu Parishad (VHP) and one of the more crude fascists even by the standards of his own organization, proved rather more prescient: "The Hindutva laboratory has started functioning," he exulted, "the BJP has won all the three seats in the Rajasthan Assembly by-elections too. A Hindu Rashtra can be expected in the next two years . . . we will change India's history."

Only one of Togadia's "two years" has passed so far and in December 2003, a year after the Gujarat elections – and almost exactly eleven years after the destruction of the Babri Masjid – the Sangh Parivar has repeated that feat in three more states, contiguous states one might add – spectacularly in Madhaya

Pradesh and Rajasthan and a bit less spectacularly than that in Chhattisgarh: a widespread repetition of Gujarat nevertheless, on a wider geographical scale, creating something of a miniature Hindu Rashtra in west-central India. If the ratio of seats between BJP and the Congress was 126 to 37 in Gujarat, it was 173 (up from 83) to 38 (down from 124) in Madhya Pradesh, and 120 (up from 33) to 56 (down from 153) in Rajasthan. That they have done it without another pogrom – that Uma Bharati can become chief minister in India's largest territorial state and can turn the swearing-in ceremony into something of a Hindutva religious ritual and a VHP political takeover without firing a shot, without even running a hate campaign – is in itself rather frightening; Gujarat has been normalized retrospectively and the far right can now occupy centre stage, led by a bloodthirsty sanyasin in MP and a dynastic princess in Rajasthan, while sections of the liberal media simply sing praises of what it describes as "woman power." Poor Sheila Dikshit, sandwiched between Uma Bharati and Vasundara Raje Scindia, as a "woman", just like them, in mediatic representations covering the whole range of the effete, upper class journals and telecasts; no Hindutva, no contests against Hindutva, no ideology, no politics, just a political sorority! India Today, for example, published an ORG-MARG poll showing that 53 percent of "housewives" voted for Uma Bharati in MP against 30 per cent for Digvijay Singh and 59 percent for Sheila Dixit in Delhi against 35 percent for Khurana, and drew the conclusion that "the key to the poll results has been the unprecedented wave of women voters rooting for women leaders over men" (15 December 2003). Most poll analysts emphasized Bharati's and Raje's commitment to "development," BJP's adroit use of caste equations, local issues, micro-management of the electoral campaign, and so on.

Immediately after the polls, Vajpayee asserted vehemently that the issue of Hindutva was simply absent from the contests. In a sense he was right. It was BJP's opponents – the so-called secular parties outside the Left who avoided that issue. If the Congress had made a bid to take part of the Hindu communal vote in Gujarat by inducting Vaghela, Digvijay Singh re-made himself and competed with Uma Bharati to show that he was as much of a Hindu devotee as her and even more devoted to cow protection; Bharati was not a good enough Hindu, he said, because her cake had eggs in it. Samajwadi Party (SP) – led by the man whom the Hindutva brigade used to call 'Maulana Mulayam' – entered into an understanding with the BJP and won an unprecedented seven seats in MP where it otherwise had little presence. By contrast, the BJP's entire electoral drive was so focused on consolidating the RSS/VHP power that it need not have raised the issue of Hindutva and was indeed grateful that its main adversary did not raise it either.

Vasundhara Raje has inherited the mantle of her mother who was an illustrious patron of the Sangh parivar. Uma Bharati is, in her own generation, perhaps the most illustrious figure associated with the Babri masjid demolition. Raman Singh and Dilip Singh Judev, who competed for chief ministership of Chattisgarh, are RSS veterans. Narendra Modi himself was a star speaker and is said to have drawn crowds larger than Vajpayee himself could; he was the most prominent presence on stage at Raje's swearing-in ceremonies. As in Gujarat, these electoral campaigns were tightly controlled on the ground by the RSS/VHP cadres, and many volunteers associated with these outfits were brought in from Gujarat and Maharashtra. RSS has long been working in the tribal belts in all three states and BJP finally cashed in on that work, winning 77 of the 99 constituencies reserved for the scheduled tribes there. In the Bastar region of Chhattisgarh, for example, Congress had 10 seats out of 12 but now has none. In Rajasthan, BJP won 26 of the 33 seats reserved for Scheduled castes while the Congress tally came down from 31 to 5. In Madhya Pradesh, the Congress share of the adivasi vote fell from 60 percent to 40 percent. Indeed, caste analysis of the BJP vote shows a wide spread all the way from princely families to the powerful Jat lobby in Rajasthan, and from a variety of upper castes to OBCs and masses of adivasis across the three states, all led by a new generation of hard-core Hindutva functionaries.

Alongside these electoral victories for the BJP, the Congress-NCP state government in Maharashtra is tottering, and the RSS/VHP/Bajrang Dal combine has launched massive mobilizations in Karnataka; their Virat Hindu Samajotsav in Bangalore in December 2003 is said to have drawn upward of 50,000 to listen to Togadia's venomous rants. Repeating the model of the Ayodhya campaigns in UP and the Bhojshala agitation in MP, the Sangh Parivar is focusing in Karnataka on the Bababudangiri shrine in Chikmagalur, demanding that the ecumenical sufi dargah be turned into a Hindu temple. The ruling Congress government in the state has characteristically responded by allowing all these agitations and providing security for them, in pursuit of its own 'soft hindutva' line as it contemplates its chances of survival in the assembly elections due next year – that same line that has brought it to grief elsewhere.

A survey conducted by the Centre for the Study of Developing Societies (CSDS) before the elections showed that majority of the electorate was in fact satisfied with the performance of Congress state governments in Delhi, Rajasthan and Chhattisgarh; only in Madhya Pradesh had Digvijay Singh made such a mess of public facilities – notably roads, power supply and electricity rates –

that he was likely to be thrown out. However, only in Delhi did that popular satisfaction with the performance of government translate itself into votes. What, then, explains the debacle in Rajasthan and Chhattisgarh and the size of the defeat in Madhya Pradesh? Splintering of the non-BJP vote was surely a factor; even in Madhya Pradesh, all the seven SP victories were at the expense of the Congress. Had there been a united fight against the BJP, that united force would have won in Chhattisgarh and Rajasthan would have had at least a hung assembly. Then there was the money; Vasundhara Raje alone is known to have spent 8 crores. And BJP is no longer associated with any particular segment of the caste spectrum; it cut into the Congress vote all the way from Brahmins and Thakurs to the Schedules castes and tribes. Above all, the massive shift of the adivasis was surely decisive. Congress had more or less monopolized this vote for fifty years. By now, the RSS has worked tirelessly among them for well over a decade through a variety of its front organizations while Congress governments, specially in Madhya Pradesh, did nothing to either counter that propaganda and mobilization nor for contributing to the security and progress of adivasis; indeed, government-appointed police and forest officials were seen as primary agents of repression while RSS fronts often provided the counterweight and in the process did their work of saffronising the tribal identity.

In all this electoral calculus, one simply cannot ignore the real and widespread hold of the Hindutva factor. Uma Bharati is not just another BJP leader. She, with her saffron robes and shaven head, embodies and personifies hard-core Hindutva without, at this late stage of her public career, having to make vitriolic speeches. Narendra Modi, the star vote-getter, is not just another Chief Minister from a neighbouring state; he represents the bloodlust of the Sangh parivar. Truckloads of RSS, VHP, Bajrang Dal cadres were brought in from Gujarat and Maharashtra not just because they have experience in running electoral campaigns. They carried with them a certain kind of macho, aggressive, murderous personality which the new, saffronised political culture accepts and admires; they are the carriers and exporters of the Gujarat model. Not for nothing did the RSS keep the campaign planning tightly under its control, and not for nothing did Sudarshan himself hold tutorial sessions for the BJP MLAs immediately after the elections.

On the morrow of these defeats, a consoling thought has begun doing the rounds in liberal, secular circles: that the BJP already has a large number of MPs in the current parliament from these states so that its victories in the assembly elections shall not make much difference to the forthcoming Lok Sabha elections. That may be so. But the numbers from even these states can surely go up, and the demonstration effect of these Hindutva victories is already palpable in Maharashtra and Karnataka. This effect can only strengthen the BJP-TDP alliance in Andhra Pradesh, while Jayalalitha's self-saffronisation proceeds apace and her re-entry into the NDA now seems to be a matter of time only. In the worst case scenario, which is not altogether implausible, we may soon have a situation in which Kerala remains the sole exception and all the other states of the south as well as western and central India are held by the BJP and its allies, in addition to states in the north and east, in a huge swath arching from Orissa to Goa and from Rajasthan to Karnataka. No one can quite tell what the fallout shall be in Bihar and what would be Mulayam's calculations in UP; his tacit current understanding with BJP there and more overt adjustment with it in MP is fraught with future uncertainties as to his eventual drift.

All this is bound to weave itself into the Lok Sabha elections where BJP may well improve its tally to become even more dominant within the NDA. Meanwhile, the character of the BJP itself is changing, as it becomes the party of rule, a new generation takes over, VHP ceases to be a rabble-rousing side show to become an electoral force pushing the ruling party directly, and as hardcore Hindutva becomes part of the mainstream equations of power. The Vajpayees and the Advanis belong to an RSS generation that spent much of its life in political obscurity; the Pramod Mahajans and the Arun Jaitleys, the Modis and the Togadias, the Bharatis and the Rajes came to prominence with the Ayodhya movement itself and have only known an RSS fraternity that has gone from power to more power to more power. With them, the specifically Indian variety of fascism comes of age.

The above narrative recalls some of the salient points I have offered in two of the essays collected in this volume. First, I have argued that never in history has the far right come to power on its own; it initially comes to power, rather, when the left gets isolated and the liberal centre collapses, parts of it submitting itself to the dominance of the far right and other parts rendering themselves ineffectual through internecine quarrels and a politics of opportunism and incoherent tactics without any overall strategy of frontal confrontation. Second, it is the failure of the liberal order to offer radical solutions for mass misery which paves the way for the far right to make inroads among the immiserated – the wretched of this earth – with millenarian promises and to organize them into a fighting force under its own cultural and political hegemony; the experience of misery does not necessarily lead anyone to a politics of the left, it may equally well lead one to a politics of the radical right; all that depends on the organizational skills, resourcefulness and perseverence of those who do the organizing. No serious student of fascism would be surprised to see that, in the absence of a left challenge, it is the fascist right that has gained so massively among the adivasis; even a saffronised Hindu identity which comes with promises of power is very consoling for the powerless whose tribal identity is so widely despised and exploited. Third, the inherent advantage of the RSS is that it has built itself into a tightly-knit cadre organization and a fraternity of overlapping fronts run by its seasoned cadres, and that it represents a specific and comprehensive world-view – call it 'culture' if you will – which gives to its members and affiliates a sense of political belonging, social coherence, even a sense of their place in the cosmos; something that the haphazard politicking of the contemporary liberal order in India, with a sense of neither direction nor mission, cannot match.

Fourth, this world-view, strongly "culturalist" as it is, is also a comprehensive program of the Right: break-neck privatisation and liberalisation, far-reaching integration of domestic capital with foreign corporate capital in a relationship of subordination, relaxing of the taxation and revenue regimes for the propertied classes, comprehensive attack on the working class including an attack on hard-won rights such as the right of government employees to strike, re-alignment of foreign and defence policies with far right forces on the global scale, such as Israel and the United States, and so on. This combination of saffronisation and neoliberalism is thus a comprehensive attempt to dismantle the very principles and visions upon which the Republic was initially founded: a full-scale counterrevolution of sorts.

The first two essays in this collection analyse these issues at greater length, and I have used the introductions both to the first and the second editions of this collection to update the factual narrative. The third essay 'Globalization and Culture' puts forward certain initial theses about the nature of imperialism today which have been much re-worked and elaborated in a later, much lengthier essay, 'The Imperialism of Our Time', which can be found in my new book, *Afghanistan, Iraq and the Imperialism of Our Time*, which is currently in the press for LeftWord Books.

I am grateful to my friends Nalini Taneja and Asad Zaidi for considering this collection worthy of a reprint and for having waited almost a whole year for this new introduction.

Introduction to the First Edition

The three essays collected in this short volume were written over a period of some eight years and represent a small but perhaps representative selection of my recent writings on the issue of communal fascism and, more obliquely, the nature of imperialism in our time. Implied in this juxtaposition of two texts on communalism and one on globalization is the suggestion that there is a structural even though not a causal connection between the current fascist offensive in India which passes itself off as Hindu nationalism, the new imperialist offensive which passes itself off as 'globalization', and the immense brutalisation of culture and politics that we are witnessing at present on the national as well as global scale. Within India, a historic shift toward neoliberal economic policies coincided with the onset of a historically unprecedented communal offensive that was initiated with the destruction of the Babri Masjid in an orgy of violence that had all the classic features of a fascist spectacle. However, this sea-change within India also corresponded, chronologically and structurally, to three fundamental shifts on the global scale: the destruction of the Soviet Union and final dissolution of the socialist project in southeastern Europe, the outbreak of powerful fascist movements across the world, and a global triumph of neo-liberalism. What has been happening in India since the late 1980s is not *caused* by the new imperialist offensive on the world scale in some direct, linear way; but it is not unconnected either.

"On the Ruins of Ayodhya" is chronologically the first of these essays and was drafted in December 1993, a year after the Ayodhya vandalism, in an attempt to think about the new ascendancy of the RSS theoretically and historically, not as a passing aberration but as an offensive of the far right which arose out of the actual crises of Indian polity during the last quarter of the twentieth century. Almost a decade later, I no longer subscribe to every word of that text and I have refined the argument considerably in some other, later texts. However, most of the fundamental coordinates of my thought on the issue of the rise of communal fascism to dominance in India are here.[1]

"Right-Wing Politics and the Cultures of Cruelty" came some six years later and sought to extend that earlier argument in a very specific way, by trying to think of the so-called Hindu nationalism of the RSS not only in relation to the crises of Indian politics in late 20th century but also to the chequered, contradictory history of nationalist ideologies as such, as nationalism first developed in Europe in early 19th century, as European fascism of early 20th century grew out of the ideology that was first called 'integral nationalism' , as well as the more conservative, culturalist, Brahminical strands in Indian nationalism itself, dating back to the late 19th century.[2] Again, the attempt was to connect the immediate, specific events of our time to deeper structures of history and to see the RSS offensive not as an epiphenomenon but as part of the history of bourgeois irrationalism which secular, rationalist movements of the radical Enlightenment and revolutionary Marxism have had to face again and again, in various parts of the world, over the past two hundred years.

The third of these essays, "Globalization and Culture", attempts to take up the other end of this dialectic of our times, namely the new phase of the imperialist offensive which is the overall context for the rise of movements of the far right in a number of particular countries, from the former Yugoslavia to Algeria to India, not to speak of half a dozen countries in Western Europe itself.[3] Departing from the conventional view of the so-called 'Globalization' as an effect merely of information technologies and increasingly integrated world markets – a view not entirely wrong but very partial owing to its economistic mystification and technological determinism – I try to offer an integrated view of the process as a new phase in the history of imperialism that arises out of very complex processes of modern history and which seeks a vast global restructuring in all areas of economy, politics and culture. Cultures of cruelty upon which the communal offensive in India rests are themselves seen, then, as part of the brutalisation of culture and politics by this new imperialism. I might add that this is still an initial text, and others are likely to follow so as to fill out an argument that has been presented here in a more or less telegraphic fashion.

II

This is not the place to rehearse or condense the arguments that shall be found in this little collection. A few clarifications may be in order, however, and I shall organize them around four words that are used and abused quite frequently: communalism, nationalism, fascism, and culture.

By 'communalism' I would mean, at the very least, a fictive ethno-religious political ideology which (a) denies centrality of differences – gender and class differences, caste hierarchies, regional and linguistic distances, sectarian conflicts within a belief system – among peoples co-existing within the broad spectrum of a particular religious identification (Islam, Hinduism, or whatever); (b) denies, minimizes and/or actively fights against the extent to which these respective belief systems and their manifestations may have been in practice influenced or modified by each other (e.g. syncretic beliefs, shared forms of popular ritual and religious festivity, cultural and artistic forms, linguistic practices); (c) absolutises ritual and cultural differences between religious communities and offers historically charged narratives of primordial antagonisms; and (d) presumes, for the present and retrospectively for the long historical past, that a discrete religious community, so constructed, is, and has always been, a distinct political community as well, always at odds with other such communal entities. This is the extreme form which aptly describes the communalism as it is practised by the RSS fraternity. Two cognate points nevertheless need to be added. First, whether we look at the Muslim communal separatism which led to the creation of Pakistan or at the majoritarian communalism of the RSS, this extreme kind of communalism tends always to present itself as a nationalism, precisely because it seeks to not only restructure relations between the political communities thus conceived, but also to re-structure the nature of the nation-state itself; RSS is not only anti-Muslim but also anti-communist, hostile to the legacies of the secular national movement, and devoted to re-defining Indian nationalism through a hysterical kind of religiosity in such a way that this nationalism ceases to be anti-imperialist, comes to rest on an identification of Hindu religion and Indian culture, and makes far-reaching alliances with imperialism in particular and rightwing regimes across the globe more generally (witness the close cooperation between India and Israel under the Hindutva brigade). Second, this extreme form of communalism comes to have popular legitimacy among a considerable section of the population only when it can surround itself with softer versions of communalism within its own ranks and fellow-travellers; wins over considerable sections of the politically powerful classes to its side; is able to draw upon preceding traditions of political ideology that sustain some of its founding ideas without being identified with communalism in the imagination of the educated middle classes; and practises fascistic violences within a broader culture of cruelties in which violence against broad strata of the working people, oppressed castes and women is part of the daily routines of social life. At one end of the spectrum, then, burning the properties of Muslims comes easy to those who are used to burning the huts of agricultural workers; and gang rape of a Muslim woman is only one step away from throwing acid on your own wife because she did not bring enough dowry. At the other end of the spectrum, one has the extraordinary phenomenon of Mr. Vajpayee who can play every note in the communal repertoire and who can be quite openly a devoted servant of the RSS and the favourite prime minister of an immense cross-section of the population, especially the urban middle classes and much of the liberal media. Any plausible explanation of communalism must address this whole range of its possibilities. Nor can the success of communalism be read back from its own authenticist claims. The fact that RSS remained a marginal formation for some fifty years (1925-75), then gained a respectable position in Indian politics for the first time during the Emergency and its immediate aftermath, and has enjoyed a sustained forward march since the late 1980s requires not an analysis of its ideology alone but a historical account of shifts in Indian politics more generally which would then explain the sea-change in its own fortunes.

Because the Hindutva agenda exceeds purely communal pursuits and seeks to recaste the nation-state as a whole, and because it has so far operated within a (admittedly low-intensity) democratic order, testing the limits of that order but not breaking with it decisively, there has been a tendency in some leftwing scholarship on the subject to say that it is neither a communalism, in the narrow sense, nor anything as anti-democratic as a fascism but the ideology of a 'Hindu nationalism'. In my view, this amounts to accepting Hindutva's description of itself, castigating it merely for its majoritarianism, and evading the question as to what *kind* of nationalism it is. It also amounts to an implied notion that if you are a nationalist you cannot be a fascist, and vice versa.

This kind of confusion rests, I believe, on certain misconceptions about the very idea of nationalism as such. In the specific conditions of India, nationalism came to be identified so thoroughly with anti-colonialism and then with the democratic, secular, 'socialistic' nation-building projects on the morrow of independence that we tend to think that this is the only kind of nationalism available. In reality, the question of nationalism is as old as the first emergence of the nation-state form in modern capitalism, and the identification of nationhood with race or religion is, in many nationalist ideologies, older and sturdier than the identification of 'nation' with a shared citizenship across racial or religious differences.

There was a time in bourgeois Britain when Catholics were not allowed to live within the precincts of London, and slavery of the black race was the norm in the Americas till the later half of the nineteenth century. It is only in the very modern traditions descended from the radical Enlightenment that everyone born in a territorial nation-state has been regarded as an *equal* citizen irrespective of class, gender, creed, race or caste. Very powerful traditions in nationalist thought, notably in conservative and fascist ideologies, have been based on the idea of *preferential* citizenship for certain religious or racial and/or cultural groups over others. Both fascism and zionism are classic examples of a rightwing, irrationalist cultural nationalism built around the identification between nation and/or race and religion. Anyone who identifies Hindutva with 'Hindu nationalism' must identify it with a particularly fascistic kind of nationalism which has an identifiable lineage in modern global politics.

Which brings us, then, to the question of 'fascism' itself. Detailed comment on this matter shall be found within these essays. Three points, in brief, need to be stressed. One, ideologies and movements of the fascist type have been a punctual feature of the imperialist period and they have arisen in scores of countries across the globe, in the advanced as well as the backward countries, the colonizing European ones as well as the colonies, in all the continents and in all phases over the past century or more. Second, Nazi Germany and fascist Italy were the most successful instances and therefore became the central inspiration among such movements since the 1920s, including the RSS; but they are by no means the only 'models'. Indeed, Indian communal fascism should be studied in relation as much to the other fascist movements of the Third World as to the European ones; in relation to the *general* tendency rather than to particular 'models'. Third, I wish to repeat the truism I once coined: "every country gets the fascism that it deserves." In other words, although a general phenomenon across the world and over a century or more, fascism nevertheless takes a very specific form in any given country, in accordance with its particular historical formation. In historical analysis, understanding of the particular is greatly enriched by understanding of the general; and the general can only be fully grasped, in the last instance, in the whole, nuanced and contradictory unity of the particular. Or, to put it differently, the question is not: does the communal fascism of the RSS correspond fully to that of the Nazis? The question, rather, is: what would fascism look like if it ever came to India?

Finally, Culture. This is probably one of the most difficult words in the English language and there is really no way of explicating it in a brief comment. In most usages, culture is identified with higher learning and the arts. National culture therefore comes to be identified with what is generally considered to be its great achievements in such areas as philosophy, music, poetry, the plastic arts, aesthetics, science, religion, and cultivated taste for such achievements. In societies divided by caste and class, this 'national culture' comes to be identified with the culture of the upper classes and tends to incline toward classicism and conservatism; Indian culture is great because it gave us the Upanishads, Kalidas and so on. I tend to use the word in a different sense, as the lived experience of a people, as practical consciousness and what Gramsci craftily called 'common sense' and which interpenetrates with the Marxist idea of 'dominant ideology'; but also something *divided*, as class society itself is divided; as something over which contests, including very bloody contests, take place, as relations between classes and castes are fundamentally contestatory; the life of sense and sensibility as it is actually, concretely lived, but a thing *distorted*, since it is a fundamental project of both capitalism to distort and deform the sensibility of the oppressed themselves—to *colonise* their unconscious and turn them not only into victims but also (sometimes unwilling but at other times willing) into agents of its own cruelties. Recovery of a culture of resistance from underneath the weight of that culture of cruelty is a specific task of the Left.

III

I am grateful to my friends Nalini Taneja and Asad Zaidi for thinking up the idea of bringing these three essays together into a short, not so expensive book. They still contain what strikes me as some useful starting-points for thinking about communalism and imperialism in our time. I would have been much happier if they had ceased to have any such relevance. That would have been the case if Hindutva had been defeated and the imperialist penetration of our society and economy warded off. That, unfortunately, is not the case. Both are more menacing than ever.

As I draft this introduction in early June 2002, the country has gone through a period of roughly six months in which we have been subjected to the largest and most prolonged peacetime military mobilisation that any country has witnessed since World War II as well as a fully fledged pogrom in Gujarat which even the investigating team of the European Union has been constrained to describe as "ethnic cleansing" and to compare it with the events of the 1930s in Germany. We have witnessed the Supreme Court thwarting the VHP's attempt to start building a temple in the immediate vicinity of the demolished Babri Masjid even as the country's Attorney General, Soli Sorabji, argued in favour of the VHP, and we have also witnessed Vajpayee retaliating by sending a functionary of his Prime Minister's Office to personally receive, on behalf of the government, the *shila* offered by Ramchandra Das Paramhans in order, in the words of BJP spokesman V. K. Malhotra, to give "sanctity" to the ritualistic inauguration. How a functionary of the PMO can bestow "sanctity" on what purports to be a religious ceremony remained unclear, but it was clearly an indication of the government's resolve to help build that temple regardless of the fact that the matter is in the Supreme Court which may yet deny construction. This violation of the very spirit of the Supreme Court order was in keeping with Mr. Vajpayee's own declaration in parliament on 6 December 2000 that the building of the Ram temple was an "expression of the national sentiment" and a task that had remained "unfinished". Three days later, on 18 March, the draconian Prevention of Terrorism Act (POTA) was passed in the Lok Sabha with a comfortable majority, 261 to 137, paving the way for its swift passage through a joint session of the two houses of parliament, with an equally comfortable majority of 129 votes. It thus replaced the more provisional Prevention of Terrorist Acts Ordinance (POTO). The timing was significant in the perspective of Gujarat and, indeed, POTO itself had been used there against Muslims but not Hindus.

At no time during these events did the so-called 'secular allies' of the BJP inside and outside the National Democratic Alliance care to invoke the National Agenda for Governance (NAG) which is said to be the programmatic basis for the NDA alliance and which forbids constituent parties to take unilateral action on controversial issues generally and on Ayodhya in particular. This direct collusion of its so-called 'secular allies' became depressingly clear during the parliamentary debate on the Gujarat holocaust which took place just when the BSP-BJP alliance was being cemented in U.P., on April 30th. The horrific barbarity that one heard from the BJP and some of its allies, notably the insufferable George Fernandes, has been covered in the media at length and has provoked protests from women's organisations in particular. Other allies were notable for the repugnant duplicity of first playing to the gallery by delivering mournful speeches on the issue of the Gujarat killings and then calmly voting in solidarity with the BJP on the actual motion. BSP was predictably part of this charade. And then there was the pathetic case of Omar Abdullah, who resigned from his post as junior cabinet minister before he rose to speak, got his National Conference MPs to abstain on the vote, and then quickly returned to his post as Minister of State for Foreign Affairs, as if the spectre of Gujarat had just been exorcised by a pretty speech. Unsurprisingly, the government won by 276 to 182 votes, with eight abstentions.

Much else has happened during these months to greatly accelerate the forward March of Hindutva, as was evident in the unopposed selection of Manohar Joshi, the notorious Shiv Sainik, to the Speakership of Lok Sabha even as BJP has its Prime Minister. It is perhaps befitting that the short period of six months that we are reviewing here and which began with the largest peacetime military mobilisation in modern history should culminate in NDA's nomination as well as the willing acceptance, by not just the NDA allies but also the Congress and the Samajwadi Party, of Mr Abdul Kalam, a nuclear freak and a super-hawk, to the Presidency of the Republic. The left was isolated on this matter as in so many other.

The first thing to be said in this regard is that Mr. Kalam's main expertise is in missile technology, and that his extraordinary dedication to the creation of weapons of mass destruction is his sole claim to fame and eminence. He has no other achievement to his credit. Nor is it at all clear why a man who administers such a program should be called "a great scientist". What about those who have rendered similar 'patriotic' services to *their* government in Pakistan? Are they also "great scientists"? Why not? And those who gave us Hiroshima and Nagasaki? What would we say, for example, if the shoe was on the other foot and Dr. Qadeer, the "father" of the Pakistani bomb, were to be made President of that country? The prospect of Mr. Kalam getting elevated to an office that was designed to symbolise the moral and visionary side of Indian national aspirations is a precise measure of the distance the nation has travelled since those innocent times when Gandhi had held out the promise of a non-violent India, Nehru had formulated the Panchsheel principles and Sarvepalli S. Radhakrishnan had occupied this august office.

BJP's reasons for choosing him are ignoble and if he had the moral fibre that is befitting a President of this Republic he should have declined. First, BJP didn't really want him. Krishna Kant came close to be chosen but was then discarded because, with his chamelion-like character, he simply could not be trusted to do the RSS bidding; nor could the Congress be predicted to join the consensus. Alexander seems to have been their real favourite but the fear was, as rumour has it, that President Naraynan himself might have stood and given a fight over the question of communalism and secularism. So, Abdul Kalam became their nominee by default. Second, having a Muslim who otherwise has no standing and is therefore expected to do as he is told was convenient in the aftermath of the ethnic cleansing in Gujarat.

That ongoing holocaust has not only shocked many sections of the Indian population but, more crucially, brought the RSS veterans to a point where there may soon be cases in European courts asking for extradition not only of Modi but also Vajpayee and Advani for "crimes against humanity". These gentlemen are on their way to perhaps becoming international pariahs, like Ariel Sharon who has for years avoided landing on European soil for fear of getting arrested as a war criminal. Abdul Kalam can be their fig leaf, the badge of their pseudo-secularism.

This is not the place to comment at any length on the complexities and dangers of the present situation. I have cited these few instances of RSS aggressivity in recent past to illustrate the extent to which it is now bent on accelerating the realisation of its own agenda, and the extent also of the active collusion of virtually all the political parties outside the Left. It is significant that Congress opposed the BJP neither in the case of the Speakership nor of the Presidency. It merely hoped that the BJP would grant it the Vice President's post, for which of course it has been summarily rebuffed. Let me simply close with the regretful remark that the trends I had identified in these essays seem to have become even much stronger than I had feared for the short term, and we are already faced with the classic situation of a pre-fascist upheaval. What used to be the political centre has collapsed, with the Congress reduced to parliamentary minority and mendicancy, and all the rest so splintered as to be assimilated into support for the fascist project as small, ineffectual groupings. BJP rules on the strength of its own inner cohesion and the obedience of those splinters in the first instance; the machinery of terror in the hands of fraternal organisations such as the VHP and Bajrang Dal, in the second instance; sufficiently large proportion of the state personnel and the priviliged professional strata allied with it, in the third instance; rapid changes in the social and cultural environment which favour its ideological positions, in the fourth instance; and, negatively, the isolation and relative weakness of the Left and the labour movement, in the fifth instance. All this is happening in an international environment far more conducive to forces of the Right and the Far Right on the global scale. Vajpayee is no more a man of the Right than George Bush; Modi looks almost benign in comparison with Ariel Sharon; RSS-style parties of the Far Right are gaining in strength in any number of countries in Europe. Those who have demanded the banning of jehadi outfits in Pakistan in the name of a "war against terrorism" will never demand the banning of VHP and Bajrang Dal on the same grounds, rivers of the blood of innocents in India notwithstanding, because our terrorists are pro-imperialist. Such are the dark times in which one has to keep up the struggle!

Notes

1 This essay was first drafted for presentation at a workshop in Hyderabad on the first anniversary of the destruction of Babri Masjid, was subsequently revised for publication in *Social Scientist* and then again for publication in my book *Lineages of the Present* (Delhi, Tulika, 1996; London, Verso, 2000).

2 Chronologically the second of these three essays, it is comprised of only a slightly revised version of a lecture given in February 1999 in memory of the late Ved Gupta, one of the key founders of the Democratic Teachers Front (DTF), also *Lineages*, then published in *Social Scientist* and then very substantially re-written for inclusion in the Verso edition of *Lineages*.

3 A very rudimentary version of a couple of these ideas was first presented at the Zentrum Mederner Orient in Berlin in September 2000 and incorporated in a *Frontline* essay (October 13,

2000). The argument was then fully developed first in a lecture I gave in Delhi some three months later in memory of Safdar Hashmi and in a presentation for People's Conference Against Globalization, also in Delhi, in March 2001. Various versions of it have since been delivered as lectures at Jawaharlal Nehru University, Oxford and Berkley. Safdar Hashmi Memorial Lecture was published in *Nukkar*, a publication of Jan Natya Manch (JANAM).

On the Ruins of Ayodhya

Communalist Offensive and Recovery of the Secular[1]

As images of the mass hysteria that accompanied the wanton destruction of that obscure little mosque in Ayodhya were flashed, over and again, in the mass media, I was surely not the only one who saw in it not an event of inter-denominational strife – in other words, a 'communal' act – but a fascist spectacle, in the classic sense.[2] There was, first of all, the audacity of it: a huge mob trained and assembled by the fronts of the RSS, including the Bharatiya Janata Party (BJP), the second largest political party in the country, openly set out to destroy what the highest court of law in the land had sought to protect through all the force at the disposal of the state and central governments, on a piece of land located within the state ruled by the self-same BJP whose key leaders were present to bless the destruction. What was visually the most striking, however, was the immaculately methodical staging of mass hysteria and the orgiastic destruction; the spectacle had been most carefully prepared but then released with the force of a hurricane that left much of the country simply stunned.

As a secular intellectual, I experienced in the destruction of a mosque neither the feeling of a religious hurt nor any sense of a clash or crisis of identities. I did then, and I still do, regard that event as a fascist assault on the Indian Constitution, a matter far more grave than the issue of denominational identities. In a lecture I wrote up soon after that event and which I delivered in Calcutta towards the end of December 1992,[3] I had argued, alongside some reflection on Gramsci, that a potential for fascist resolutions is particularly strong in those semi-industrialized societies such as ours which have inherited powerful traditions of classicism, cultural conservatism, and authoritarian religiosity, and which have failed to undertake revolutionary transformations of cultural life and a radical redistribution of material resources. The present text is in some ways a continuation of that argument, but with far more direct reference to our present predicament. The question with which I should want to begin these reflections is this: was it only in the heat of that macabre moment that one had felt the palpable presence of the spectre of fascism, or is it still legitimate, and in what sense could it be legitimate, to speak of 'fascism', a very loaded word indeed, in this context? In posing this question, moreover, I want to assume that most of the basic facts about the career and composition of the Sangh parivar are generally quite well known,[4] so that the argument may proceed mainly on an analytic level.

A great problem in raising such a question is that discussions of fascism tend to get bogged down in the issue of analogies and paradigms. There is a more or less paradigmatic description of fascism that is derived largely from the Nazi experience (even Italy comes up in India very rarely and for secondary consideration only) so that all other movements that seem to belong to this analytic category tend then to be compared with the German paradigm in all sorts of ways, to be judged as to how truly fascist they are; predictably, most are found wanting in one respect or another. This procedure strikes me as being faulty. Every country gets the fascism that it deserves, i.e., the historical form of fascism always shifts according to the historical, economic, political, social, even religious and racial physiognomy of a given country, and it is useless always to seek an approximation with the German experience. In its heyday during the years between the two world wars, fascism triumphed in few enough countries but it was a general tendency throughout Europe, taking quite different forms and reaching quite distinct ends in different countries; and European fascisms inspired a whole host of related movements around the globe, from Latin America to the Middle East to Japan. In our own time also, fascistic movements are arising across the globe, even though the word 'fascism' has by now fallen in such disrepute that hardly any one of such movements likes to refer to itself by that word; the Italian one continued to use that designation for itself for some decades, then called itself 'post-Fascist' for a while, then abandoned the word altogether, and eventually settled on a more innocuous self-description, as 'National Alliance'. It seems more appropriate, therefore, to begin not with an abstract paradigm to be applied to specific movements but to examine the basic structure, actions, and objectives of a particular movement – in our case, Hindutva in general and RSS and/or Shiv Sena in particular – to see whether or not it can be judged as being fascist in the proper sense of the word.

The logical structure of the present text arises out of this very principle. In the opening sections, I offer some analytic comments on the fascistic nature of the actions, organizational principles, ideological formulations, and programmatic objectives of Hindutva. This leads to a detailed consideration of the specific political conjuncture in India, arising from the demise of the Congress hegemony by the mid-1970s, for the dramatic rise to prominence on the part of Hindutva forces that had been languishing on the margins of the polity since the 1920s. It is in this context that certain comparative remarks are offered, briefly about the classic Fascist experience of Italy and Germany before the Second World War, but then in more detail about the right wing Islamicist radicalisms of the past two decades with which Hindutva can be more fruitfully compared. I close, then, with a longish excursus on the history and trajectory of secularism which, I believe, has been historically at the very origin of the rise of democratic demand and conceptions of equality in the political and economic domain. In India, at least, it has not been possible in the past and shall not be possible in the future to uphold ideas of constitutional democracy or socialist equality without a prior politics of secular civility. The opposition between secularism and fascism, in a country such as ours, is thus not incidental but integral.

I

To start with, then, the question itself needs to be posed correctly. If we were to ask whether or not fascist rule is on the horizon in India, my answer would be: no, not in the immediate future. If we were to ask whether communalism as such is a fascism, I would say: no, not necessarily, not all communalism by any means. But, specifically with reference to the destruction of Babri Masjid and the forces that carried it out, I would say that we would forget at our peril the fundamentally fascist character of that event and those forces. This seems clear with regard to the nature of the event, the modes of mobilization, the very structure of the Sangh parivar, and the specific ideological form in which it practises and propagates its communalism – all of which makes it rather similar to Shiv Sena, on not only a much larger scale but also with a much more comprehensive and articulated structure, and distinguishes it from many other kinds of communalism. Let me briefly explain.

First, the event. As we know, BJP's legally constituted government of Uttar Pradesh, sworn to uphold the Constitution, gave a binding undertaking to the Supreme Court that it would protect the Ayodhya mosque and immediately proceeded to violate the undertaking, with ample evidence that the giving and the violating of that undertaking had been meticulously and more or less openly planned. Meanwhile, the central government, also sworn to uphold the Constitution, fully aware of the preparations, duly warned by the intelligence agencies that destruction of the mosque in defiance of the Supreme Court order was indeed part of the Hindutva plan, but following a 'soft saffron' line, did nothing to prevent that violation of the constitutional obligation. Then, after the event, the government made no move to punish the actual culprits beyond empty gestures, despite overwhelming evidence, including photographic evidence, as to the identity of those culprits, their accomplices, and their leaders.

In its internal structure, meanwhile, the destruction of the Masjid has all the characteristics of a fascist spectacle, coming on top of many preparatory spectacles, carefully calibrated over the years.[5] It displayed the familiar fascistic relationship between the parliamentary party and the extra-parliamentary wings; that same chain running from the semi-clandestine group of actual leaders of the RSS abstaining from incriminating attendance, to the leaders of the various mass fronts actually supervising the destruction, to trained cadres, to the mob – bound together by a carefully choreographed hysteria and exhortations to violence. The exhortations were replete with appeals to masculine virility, national pride, racial redemption, contempt for law and civility – so that the liberal Mr Vajpayee, the patrician Mr Advani, the deliberately shrieking Uma Bharati, and those goons of Bajrang Dal who had come to believe that they were, quite literally, monkeys in the army of Hanuman, the servants of Ram and the eventual protectors of Hindu female chastity, were joined together in a public ritual that was expected to propel the purportedly 'non-political' Sangh, through its parliamentary arm but with the muscle power of its non-parliamentary wings, to unassailable state power.

As if the event itself was not enough, video cassettes not only of the event but of many subsequent acts of violence were then distributed throughout the country, so that they could be re-lived, over and over again, vicariously, by a whole host of men throughout the land, as so many moments of regained Hindu virility, as redefined by the parivar. This is, I would contend, fascist masculinism with a vengeance. We might add that the Shiv Sena was fully involved, as a partner of the parivar, in the destruction of the mosque; that it subsequently took credit for it openly; that when the Sena went on a rampage of murder in Bombay, the parivar is said to have supplied it with lists and addresses of those whose houses and flats were to be set afire; that the big bourgeoisie of Bombay was itself so intimidated that it dared not openly call for either the banning of the Sena or the arrest of its leader and Founding Father, Bal Thackeray; and that so blatant and even self-intoxicated have the fascists become that the assassins of Gandhi are openly celebrated in cities of Maharashtra, with no reprisals.

The issue of Shiv Sena we shall here ignore. But we could go behind the destruction of the mosque and the communal orgies that came before and after it, to the self-organization of the parivar itself – and we shall be brief, since all this is familiar enough. The image of the family is crucial here, because of its patriarchal resonance, even though the strictly all-male RSS is referred to by fronts of the parivar as mata (mother). At the head we have a semi-secret, non-parliamentary organization, the Sangh itself, led by a handful of men, mostly of the brahmin caste bound by no norms of democratic representation even in principle, whose methods of internal organization, promotion, decision-making, lists of actual cadres, etc., remain shrouded in secrecy, despite the agreement under which the ban on the Sangh was lifted in the 1950s and which requires legal accountability on these issues. This is the organization which assembles the fascist structure vertically, from the shakha (branch) upward, with its organizational ethic of cadre-building, loyalty, and obedience, and its ideological identification of local community, Hindu culture with Indian nationhood; and, it organizes the structure horizontally, by spawning numerous fronts – perhaps fifty or more, as they claimed after the more recent ban in the wake of the Ayodhya vandalism – for women, children, workers, etc., but also for religious mobilization, training of terror squads, and so on. The Sangh's obvious public face is that of the BJP, supposedly a political party like the rest, but even the formation of municipal government in Delhi has shown that all the power is wielded by the RSS itself – not to speak of the Advanis, the Vajpayees, the Joshis, etc., in the central leadership, all RSS veterans. Alongside that are other semi-public faces: the VHP, the Bajrang Dal, the Dharm Sansad (Parliament of Faith), etc., to assist in parliamentary mobilization but also for non-parliamentary mobilization; for the assertion that matters of faith are not subject to law and Constitution; to concentrate requisite force to drive that message home, especially to the religious minorities but also to the country at large. In the vast space that separates – but also connects – Mr Vajpayee and the Bajrang Dal, are the intellectuals, the media manipulators, the experts in electronic fabulation, who interpret the daily events for us through newspapers; who lay out the visual images in those same newspapers to manipulate our sensory experience of what we read; who flood the mass market with films and videos. Here, too, in this sphere of ideological mobilization and remaking, there are levels and calibrations: the national network of the in-house publications of the RSS is carefully distinguished from a similarly national network of publications which represents the RSS viewpoint without being formally a part of the authorized network, which is then balanced against methodical penetration of the liberal media themselves, extending to the upper reaches of the respectable dailies. Thus, the open terrorization of journalists by the Shiv Sena in Bombay and the Sangh-Sena combine in Ayodhya is delicately balanced against the freedom of saffron ideologues to use the editorial pages of such newspapers as the Times of India to propagate their views and thereby become respectable partners in defining the agenda for national debate. As if all that wasn't enough, we have a battery of historians and archaeologists to rewrite the textbooks and fabricate a fantastic history, with a contempt for the facticity of facts that no poststructuralist in his right mind could ever hope to match.

In its staging of spectacles, in its techniques of mobilizations, in the multiplicity of its fronts, in the shadowy traffic between its parliamentary and non-parliamentary organs, in the seamless interplay of form and content in its ideological interpellations, in the connection it asserts between a resurgent national tradition and the regaining of masculinist virility, in its simultaneous claims to legality and extra-legality, in its use of religion as a kind of racialism, in its construction of a mythic history which authorizes it to be above history, and in its organization of a Dharm Sansad that authorizes it to be above the civil Parliament whenever it so chooses, the Sangh parivar is a classically fascist force – with large Indian twists of course, as every fascism must always take a specifically national form.

Because of features such as these, the Sangh represents not only a communalism, in the ordinary sense, even though minorities in general and Muslims in particular are its special victims. The true object of its desire is not mere Muslim submission but state power and the remaking of India as a whole – politically, ideologically, historically; and, true to form, this project of remaking India in its own image involves a great deal of unmaking, both through selective appropriation as well as outright rejection of very large parts of our past and present histories. This process of unmaking and remaking involves the rejection of our secular-nationalist and communist histories; the re-domestication and redefinition, in the name of 'Tradition', of what little independence some women in this country have been able to achieve; to slow down the upsurge of the dominated castes; to control the pluralities of our intellectual and cultural productions; to club the regional minorities into submission to a centralized, authoritarian state; and to bestow upon a backward bourgeoisie nostalgias of an imperial past, dreams of nuclear power, hallucinations of regional dominance. Communalism, in other words, is only a cutting edge, even though this edge is quite capable of causing bloodbaths time and again.

The Sangh foregrounds the issues of what it calls 'pseudo-secularism' and 'the appeasement of minorities' because it finds these issues strategically important in its bid to build a national consensus around a whole series of real and imagined resentments, but the object of this consensus is not merely the minority but, most centrally, that majority which we provisionally call Hindu, hence also the even more powerful project of redefining and reordering Hinduism itself, in a syndicated, monolithic, telegenic, aggressive form – part brahminical, part electronic, part plebeian. In other words, the Sangh claims and has always claimed to be a nationalism – at once the cultural nationalism of the Hindu community, and, because the community is said to be co-terminous with the nation itself, the political nationalism of the Indian people as such. The inner originary logic of this claim – part communitarian, part nationalist – is of some interest.

This logic is inherent in Golwalkar's famous distinction, as he phrased it, between his own cultural nationalism and the territorial nationalism of the Congress as led by Gandhi et al. In this formulation, cultural nationalism is the nationalism specifically of Hindus, whereas territorial nationalism is by definition secular in the sense that it includes non-Hindus as well and does not demand of them that they adopt what Golwalkar would define as Hindu culture. By this definition, it might appear that he recognizes secular nationalism as having a wider scope and the flexibility to represent all Indians, irrespective of religious affiliation, while he himself aspires to represent only the Hindus; in this sense he could be said to be the Hindu counterpart of Jinnah who eventually claimed to represent the Muslims only, leaving the Hindus to the Indian National Congress. What Golwalkar means, however, is the direct opposite: that the real Indian nation is comprised of Hindus exclusively; that Hindu cultural nationalism, which seeks to create in India not a secular polity but a Hindu Rashtra is the authentic form of Indian nationalism; that the secular, multi-denominational nationalism which seeks to include Hindus and non-Hindus alike is not only wrong and misguided but also outright unpatriotic and even anti-national; that the territorial nationhood which appears to be wider and more inclusive is in fact anti-Hindu treachery, since it denies the superiority of the Hindu majoritarian claim to the whole of this territory, where others may live only in so far as they accept the superiority of the Hindu 'race'.

To buttress this position, Golwalkar has recourse to an ideological identification between two discursive categories, *pitribhumi* (fatherland) and *punyabhumi* (spiritual homeland), worthy of German Romanticism itself, invoking the quasi-Hegelian idea of a National Spirit, representing the nation in twin images of patriarchal family and religious community, and asserting that the idea of citizenship be derived from one's active participation in the working of that Spirit. Being born an Indian is thus not enough to qualify for true citizenship because 'India' designates only a territory; the Spirit of India resides, generally, in religions that arose within India and, quintessentially, in Hinduism, so that to be a true Indian one had to be a Hindu as well; hence the insistence on the essential identity of territory with religion, and of religion with nation.

In other words, Hindus were true citizens of India prima facie by having spontaneous recourse to that National Spirit by the very fact of birth in a Hindu household, but non-Hindus could become citizens by acquiring – that is to say, submitting to – that Spirit – not as equal citizens, since nothing could compensate for the taint of inferior birth, but as a protected minority, or as wards of the state as it were. Golwalkar of course cited Nazi Germany as his model for this racialistic definition of citizenship, but what is also striking about this definition is that the purported distinction between cultural nationalism and territorial nationalism is dissolved as soon as it is made, since the entire population residing in the territory of Bharat Varsha is thereby required either to accept the cultural nationalism as defined by Hindutva or to get out. Any segment that fails to meet this requirement is invited to leave the territory altogether, on pain of extinction. The cultural nationalist, in any case, would not let go of even an inch of that territory, and would welcome, rather, the departure, even the demise, of the unwanted (because impure) segments of the population. In the more extended versions of this quasi-racialistic extremism, it is said to be the historic mission of militarized Hinduism and the Hindutva state that it would set out to recapture the territories that Greater India has lost to other states of the subcontinent, Pakistan in particular but also Bangladesh, possibly Sri Lanka, and some other neighbouring territories as well. Purification, of the existing territory, expansion into the adjacent territories of other states is thus part of the design. We might add that this design surfaces rather rarely in the rhetoric of the BJP, the parliamentary front, but surfaces more frequently in The Organizer, the tribune of the RSS, and is an open and punctual feature of the public exhortations of the non- parliamentary arms of the 'family' – the Vishva Hindu Parishad (VHP), Bajrang Dal, Durga Vahini, and others – whose muscle power and rhetorics of hate are expected to propel the respectable BJP into governmental power.

II

As regards the making of that particular form of Hinduism which the RSS presents as the cultural nationalism of the Indian people, two parallel processes of syndication are striking. The first is the familiar one for which Romila Thapar initially used the term 'syndication', whereby diverse and even conflicting practices are sought to be taken over from very different traditions and incorporated into a single, pan-Indian religiosity – a process that begins with certain strands in orientalism and for which, in the RSS version, Ram is said to be the unique, uniform godhead. This is an invented tradition, if there ever was one! But something else, and in its own way perhaps even more alarming, is that the RSS has emerged as the unique successor and a point of intersection for a great many revivalist currents which India has inherited from many quite distinct Hindu reform movements of the nineteenth century and diverse, even conflicting, political movements of the earlier decades of the present century. Vivekananda has been a staple of their invocations now for decades, and VHP's special claim to his legacy is so elaborate and strident that the forces of the liberal Left which think that they can unproblematically claim Vivekananda for a more decent formulation of the Hindu cultural ethos need to consider the consequences of that prior claim very seriously. Meanwhile, such things as the convergence between Golwalkar and Savarkar, and the later cooperation of Shyama

Prasad Mukherjee and the RSS in founding the Jan Sangh, have meant that the RSS has simply inherited the legacy of what was once the Hindu Mahasabha.[6] Even the old confrontation between the two reform movements, Arya Samajis and the Sanatan Dharmis, has largely lapsed into a somewhat syndicated rightwing Hinduism and, therefore, into a more or less singular constituency for the Sangh. Large chunks of Bankim and Aurobindo are simply rehearsed as precursors of modern-day Hindutva. Gandhi's tactic of keeping such individuals as Hedgewar and such organizations as the Mahasabha inside the Congress for as long as it remained at all possible, not to speak of the subsequent history of cooperation extended to the RSS by such diverse individuals as Sardar Patel during the Partition violence, and by Vinoba Bhave and Jayaprakash Narayan during the Bhoodan campaign to persuade landowners to give land to the landless and the anti-Indira agitation respectively, has made it all the more possible for the RSS to assert anti-colonial, reformist, even anti-authoritarian credentials. One of the notable features of this bid for building an alternative national hegemony is that the RSS lays claim, in the religious sphere, to the whole of the Hindu tradition, from the highest kind of brahminism to the most plebeian and ecumenical kind of Bhakti, as well as to the more modern kinds of revisionist Hinduism; and, in the socio-political sphere, it lays claim to the whole range of Hindu reform movements as well as to virtually every major figure in nationalist history, including Gandhi – with very few exceptions, notably Nehru and, understandably, the Muslim component of Indian nationalism. Let me note, parenthetically, that the ability of the RSS partially to co-opt the rhetoric of Gandhian socialism, Gandhian Swadeshi, Gandhian ram rajya, and their unmitigated hostility towards Nehru should give some pause to that section of our secular intelligentsia, notably the subalternists, who find it so much easier to be partial towards Gandhi but would themselves be quite as hostile towards Nehru as the RSS itself, though on somewhat different grounds. I do not mean that the priorities should simply be reversed, or that we should now set up some fundamental preference for Nehru over Gandhi in our narratives of canonical nationalism; simple reversals in such matters usually do more harm than good. What I do mean is that we need a far more careful look at those positions – frequently overlapping positions – that Gandhi and Nehru have represented within that history, even though the fashion these days, on the Right certainly but also in some sections of the radical intelligentsia, is to pitch them as opposites. After all, Gandhi's support of him was perhaps the decisive element that made Nehru the first Prime Minister of independent India; otherwise, support for Sardar Patel was probably far greater in the relevant Congress circles.

Be that as it may. Let me explore a little further my proposition that the remarkable capacity of the RSS to set its own agenda and to register a gradual but remarkably consistent expansion over a period of sixty years or more is certainly a tribute to its own organizational genius, but this genius has met with such success because of its ability to draw upon a large number of legacies which have been an enduring feature of diverse reform movements and nationalist articulations throughout the history of modern India. The idea of uniform Hindu victimization over a thousand years is as old as Indian modernity itself, and we can find it there already in Rammohun, who was otherwise also the author of Tuhfat-al-Muwahideen, a book deeply imbued with concepts of Islamic rationalism, and a pleader of the Mughal king's case in the court of the Company.

For Rammohun, of course, those were fleeting assertions, by no means a substantial part of his social or historical vision. But such ideas begin to get articulated far more systematically by the last quarter of the nineteenth century, with enough of it getting played out subsequently during the Swadeshi Movement for Tagore to warn specifically against the tendency. The pursuit of a revamped, reformed, but also monolithic and even aggressive Hinduism that presents itself as the real tradition; the invention of a past, anti-Muslim nationalism in the form of the sagas of Maratha and Rajput warriors; the idea that the kshatriya ideal of manhood is the proper ideal for Hindu manhood in general; the emphasis on physical culture and the building of the male body as a key to Hindu redemption; the figure of the heroic Sadhvi leading Hindu men in acts of redemption of the national honour – all these, and much besides, the RSS has inherited from the fictions, the zealotries, the reform movements of the nineteenth century and the twentieth, from Bengal to Maharashtra to Punjab. Its unique achievement is that ideological elements that had in the past remained discrete and largely subordinate to the requirements of an anti- colonial movement are now integrated into a singular, all- encompassing ideological position of a fascist kind and then linked, most crucially, to unique forms of organization and mobilization. Even the image of the RSS as an all-male club of reformers who know best – and that of the swamikas as both objects and agents of that reform, at once released and restrained by the reformer, active, above all, in the proper Hindu household, and then in carefully orchestrated family-to-family, neighbourhood-to-neighbourhood networks, and only very selectively on the national scene, whenever the directive agency of the reformer so desires – all this recalls, on a much grander scale of course, the quintessential relationship between the nineteenth-century reformer and the object of his reform – often the wife, the daughter, the sister-in-law. Needless to add, there is much in our secular-nationalist histories that also took over those same ideas, those same models. The secular-nationalist versions had remained essentially paternalistic and condescending, in the way of much nineteenth-century liberalism, but they have unwittingly contributed to the more aggressively masculinist versions of the RSS type.

In other words, by the time the RSS takes over such ideas, they have gathered to themselves the density of very powerful histories, no less historical for being so thoroughly modern. What I am suggesting, first, is that the difference between the so-called Hindu nationalism of the Sangh parivar and the secular nationalism of its bourgeois opponents cannot be conceptualized in the binary terms of Tradition and Modernity; the parivar itself draws upon a number of very modern traditions, and it is at least arguable that those who have choreographed its fascist spectacles, from the rath yatra onwards, know more about modernity than many of our avant garde artists and historians. But I am also suggesting, second, that the strategists of the parivar know perfectly well that many of their ideas resonate strongly with a certain kind of widespread 'common sense' that has been prepared for them already, by other movements, social practices, intellectual productions, all of which they can now selectively incorporate, by rewriting, into their own history as so many precursors of modern-day Hindutva. This is by no means the only common sense available in modern India, and it is much to be doubted that the majority of Indians subscribe to the sum of those ideas or even find them relevant. But the confidence that there is a large enough pool of consent is also visibly there, in numerous RSS practices, as for example in the stipulation that every boy who ever comes to any of the shakhas (branches) must come with prior consent and daily knowledge of elders in the family; the presumption is that the consent would already be there or can be both obtained and sustained relatively easily. Consent of course comes all the more easily not only because of prior patterns of socialization but also because the RSS, through the shakha, is able to offer facilities (such as organized sports) and particular kinds of feelings (such as pride, group bonding, social ambition) that are scarce for the majority of the children caught in the urban vortex.

But there are other kinds of consents, other kinds of violences as well, that potentially contribute to the making of a fascist project. Notable among these is the normalization of the practice of violence as a way of satisfying acquisitive desire and of imposing the will of the powerful on the powerless. An urban middle class that habitually sets its women afire because the dowry they bring does not satisfy the greed of the men of that class; because the women are not sufficiently submissive; or because they are suspected of sexual infidelity, normalizes the idea of violence as normative in gender relations. The agrarian upper castes that periodically set fire to the households of the menial castes normalize the idea of extreme violence in class and caste relations, as much as does the Indian National Congress when it carries out a pogrom in the entire Sikh community to avenge the assassination of Indira Gandhi by her bodyguard. This routinized violence is now a very considerable feature even of the tensions between those lower and middle castes and caste fractions which are upwardly mobile and those which are not, as has been increasingly evident in

Uttar Pradesh. The violence against women, which is common to all these practices of violence, stems from older and wider histories which have connected patriarchal households, caste-divided local communities and the so-called national culture in a great many complex ways. Communalism is by no means the only – and, in quantitative terms, not even the largest – structure of routine violence in our society, and there are times when a communal kind of violence comes so easily to so many men, and is exercised against even peaceful neighbours, precisely because this particular form of violence draws upon so many other kinds of aggressions. In contemporary India communalism is certainly, as I said earlier, the cutting edge for a fascist project as a whole, but those other violences – of caste, class, and gender – are always there to form the kind of authoritarian personality upon which the fascist project eventually rests.

III

The potential for a fascist condensation of such structures of violence, and for a fascist resolution for crises of such magnitude, is always there in the very structure of centralized states and coerced territorialities. But the conditions for posing the fascist alternative as a credible resolution arise only in exceptional circumstances. After all, for the first fifty years of its existence RSS could convince hardly anyone that it was worthy of ruling even a single state; and even at the height of the communal holocaust in the wake of the Partition there were few takers for the idea of Hindu Rashtra – precisely because a left-of-centre, secularist hegemony was then in place. As we look back on that history, what strikes one is that the RSS has demonstrated an astonishing pattern of calibrated growth since its inception in the late 1920s, but it is really from the 1970s, and specifically with its participation in the anti-Indira agitations spearheaded by Jayaprakash Narayan and its subsequent inclusion in the Janata Cabinet, that we can date the elevation of the Sangh to a respectable position in Indian national politics.[7] It was a propitious moment. The Congress model of capitalist accumulation had exhausted its potential by the mid-1970s; the Gharibi Hatao (Remove Poverty) campaign of Indira Gandhi was the last of those populist mobilizations that had evoked the promise of a measure of redistributive justice within the predicates of that model. The well-known leaders who had left the Congress at various points had failed either to articulate an alternative model of development or to put together a stable political organization able to challenge the Congress; the desperation of such leaders is well indicated in the fact that it was the movement led by JP and the Cabinet headed by Morarji Desai, formerly a veteran Congressman of Gandhian personal culture and rightwing political persuasion, that gave to the Sangh its respectability.[8] Meanwhile, the old CPI had been split and the ensuing Communist Parties contained in their regional electoral bases.

That was one side of the story. On the other hand, prior histories of British administration, nationalist politics, the emergence of a sovereign polity based on universal suffrage, the continuing viceregal tradition of a weak federalism under a strong centre in post- Independence India, and, above all, the stupendous growth of a national market for commodities and communications alike, with substantial increase in literacy rates and ownership of radio sets as well as the expansion of television networks, had created an objective situation for the invention of, recasting of – and contentions over – an all-encompassing, pan-Indian identity. Previous histories of the anti-colonial movement could no longer serve as the nationalist cement of society, some thirty years after Independence, unless an equally powerful anti-imperialist nationalism were to arise organically in the new conditions of a postcolonial, sovereign, developing society. But the organization of such a movement was precluded by the regional sequestration of the Left on the one hand, the demise of Nehruvian social democracy on the other. And yet, the very intensification of market relations, the rapid acceleration of communications and travel facilities, the massive elaboration of the institutional mechanisms of the nation-state, even the intricate and pyramidical workings of the political structures of electoral representations – the mechanisms, in other words, that had brought masses of Indians from diverse regions and social background into direct contact and interdependence, for the first time in the history of this civilization – objectively required a powerful ideological cement in the form of a national ideology. A national definition of the polity – in other words, a nationalist ideology – was an objective requirement of the material processes that had been unleashed by the very terms of economic and political modernity. It was in the midst of lost political hegemonies of the Centre-Left forces on the one hand, great intensification of market relations and modernization of communication systems on the other, that the RSS launched itself on its new career, after the fall of the Janata government and as the decade of the 1970s drew to a close, with a brand new parliamentary front – the collapsed Jan Sangh reborn now as the Bharatiya Janata Party – with the key non-parliamentary front, the VHP, which had been leading an obscure existence since the 1960s, waiting to be released into entirely new kinds of aggressive assertions in the 1980s.

Let me put it another way. The liberal-Left hegemony of the first two decades after Independence was based on an identifiable heritage and a solid set of achievements. Few political leaders anywhere in the modern world have commanded such hegemonic power over the social visions and even the spiritual life of so many people, as did Gandhi alone – not to speak of those, chiefly Nehru, who were seen as his associates. This, combined with the political capital associated with the leadership of the anti-colonial movement itself, gave to the Congress a unique authority in the Indian polity for a whole generation, even for those who otherwise had good reason to oppose it. Nowhere in the world, neither anywhere in Europe nor in North America, was a model of constitutional government and representative democracy, based on universal suffrage, ever introduced or stabilized with poverty levels and literacy rates as low as the ones that prevailed in India at the time of Independence. Yet, India did become a democratic society. Nowhere in the West did women gain the vote at the very inception of representative democracy; in India they did. Its sovereignty as a nation-state arose out of the crucible of a communal holocaust, yet it refused to become a Hindu Rashtra and opted, instead, to become a secular polity. This, in sharp contrast to Europe where secularism never triumphed in processes of state formation with such low levels of income and literacy. Within these politico-ideological arrangements, India during the first fifteen years after Independence witnessed the making of a largely independent model of industrial growth, a considerable reduction in the power of large-scale feudal landholdings in much of the country, substantial processes of kulakization in the countryside which benefited the upper levels of the peasantry, significant infrastructural development, expansion of educational facilities and technical personnel, etc. In other words, there was a dynamic model of embourgeoisment which at least held out the promise of some redistributive justice as well as benefits of a rapid rise in incomes for substantial sections of the population, especially at the middling levels of class formation. So long as this promise remained credible, the national bourgeoisie, under the political leadership of the reformist sections of the professional middle classes, was able to ward off challenges from the Left as well as the Right and to command the basic loyalty of the immiserated sections of society.

The dynamism of that model, and hence the belief in that promise, had begun decaying by the end of the 1960s, and victory in the Bangladesh War served to prop up that lost hegemony only provisionally and temporarily, so that when the next major challenge came to the victors, in the shape of the JP movement, they could take recourse only to the authoritarianism of the Emergency. It is indicative of the inner erosion of that earlier hegemony that the authoritarianism of that episode was utilized only to buttress personal power but not to implement a new reform package from above, as the 'progressive' supporters of the Emergency, within the radical section of the bureaucracy and even in a section of the Left, had envisaged. Instead, it was during the Emergency that the bankruptcy of the Congress model came fully into view. This of course coincided with the first major opportunity for RSS to gain political respectability and start building its own kind of hegemony out of the wreckage of the Congress model.

In short, it was the collapse of a Left-liberal kind of nationalism that provided the major opening for a fascist kind of nationalism, which set out, then, both to exploit the weaknesses of that earlier nationalism and to formulate a different national agenda. It is often suggested that an aggressive kind of political Hinduism is rising in India today because it expresses the cultural ethos of the vast majority in the country, as opposed to the secularism of the ruling elite. The experience of the first quarter-century after Independence shows that there is no such correlation. If Hinduism itself were the issue, India should have become a Hindu Rashtra in the wake of the Partition when the crisis precipitated by the Communal Award of the Partition was the most acute and when violences of denominational strife reached levels unimagined before or since; instead, the whole of the national leadership, led by Gandhi, opted for a non-denominational, modern constitutionality. That the great strides of political Hinduism began a generation later; that its fortunes have seen much ebbing and flowing in succeeding years; that it is weakest in regions where the Left is still strong but also in regions where the Muslim minorities are the weakest and the field much more open for uninterrupted Hindu cultural assertion – all this needs a more conjunctural explanation than the ahistorical one of a permanent Hindu ethos finally asserting itself.

But I want to base such an explanation on a more theoretical argument as well, namely that (1) in a developing society in which the structures of capitalism are fully in place but where processes of state formation are weakly developed and premised on acute unevennesses of region, community, and class, an ideological cement of a nationalist kind is an objective necessity; and that (2) if the Left fails to provide that cement, and if the liberal Centre begins to collapse, an aggressive kind of rightist nationalism will step into that vacuum to resolve a crisis that is produced by the objective processes of state formation and capitalist development – and this rightwing nationalism is bound to take advantage of precisely that misery of the masses and the petty-bourgeois strata which the liberal model promised to alleviate and did not. The renewed bid of the RSS to reformulate the nationalist ethos surely coincided with the erosion of that Congress model of the earlier years. It also coincided, however, with powerful processes at work in India – the processes of universal suffrage; a centralized administration; overlapping networks of regional and national education systems and print media; generalization of television and videos; the creation and constant expansion of one of the world's largest home markets for labour and commodities – that have had paradoxical effects on the formation of identities.

The integrative processes of the national market, the national system of information and communication, and the nation-state itself require the creation of a pan-Indian identity and produce the requisite conditions for such an identity formation. The intensification of democratic process and demand has had the effect, meanwhile, of creating identity not only on the singular, universal axis of citizenship but also along the multiple axes of numerous situational differences of region, locality, class, caste, language, denomination, and so on. These difficulties of reconciling the universality of citizenship in the nation-state with the situational particularity of specific identities, which is at the very heart of the democratic explosions of our time, is vastly complicated, however, by the very market mechanisms which integrate the economy of exchange and accumulation but serve to fragment the social base of that economy through the constant accentuation of competitions, inequities, and insecurities of many kinds. Indeed, the very system of administration that recruits its personnel on the national, regional, and local levels for different types of employment; the labour market that takes large masses of humanity far from home, sundering them from familiar networks of mutual dependence and hurling them, instead, into a whirlwind of monetization, with extreme insecurities of employment and income; intensities of cultural pressure that require of market agents that they have competence in languages of intra-regional communication even though they may themselves come out of regionally rooted linguistic communities – these and numerous other contradictions of market-induced integration serve to create a national identity while also propelling individuals to seek shelter from the brutalities of the national market in narrower networks of identitarian solidarities. Religion, for instance, declines absolutely as metaphysic and ethic but resurfaces, with vastly greater power, as a sign system of social recognitions which is nevertheless forever being reorganized as commerce and as denominationally competitive commodification. Community collapses into a thousand antinomies of a money economy but is invoked, with regular hysteria, as nostalgia for a past that never was and must therefore be made afresh with all the resources and ambition of a remorseless upward mobility. Caste-based politics itself becomes the ground for highly differentiated and mutually incompatible practices: struggles for justice in some places, a sanskritizing convergence of the plebeian middle castes and the brahminical personnel in other places, even the incorporation of some upwardly mobile lower and middle castes into projects of Hindutva as class fractions are recomposed across the country, under the stresses and opportunities of the market economy and the electoral process. As even a formal commitment to 'socialistic planning' was abandoned in the closing years of Indira Gandhi's government, to be replaced increasingly by a 'liberalization' that redistributes the functions of the nation-state outward to multi-national capital and multilateral agencies, and downward into the market as the ultimate arbiter of the social good, it has become less and less clear whether or not India shall in fact survive, in the long run, as a democratic federal polity comprised of very diverse regions and states-within-the-state.

Since Independence, in other words, Indian polity has experienced much restructuring and dislocation, with contradictory tendencies towards greater integrative pressures of the market and the nation-state on the one hand, greater differentiation and fragmentation of communities and socio- economic transactions on the other. As I said earlier, a national cement is an objective necessity arising out of these perplexities. But what kind of cement? Equality, it is safe to say, is the only possible ground on which the facts of social and identitarian difference can be reconciled with the demands of justice and the decencies of a universalist civilization. But equality is precisely what has receded further and further away, not only from the actual organization of society but also as the utopic horizon of aspiration upheld by the nation-state. By itself a national identity does not and need not mitigate the existence of other kinds of identities, formed at other social sites – caste, class, region, ethnicity, etc. Indeed, the proliferation of linguistic, regional, denominational or caste-based identities, combined with the extremities of class polarization in a backward capitalist society, serve only to accentuate the objective need for the strengthening of a national identity corresponding to the exigencies of the national market and the nation-state, if that market and that state are to reproduce themselves over an extended period of time. However, a developmentalist dynamic stripped of any programmatic promise of redistribiitive justice is bound to precipitate the crisis of the hyphen that equates the nation with the state in the term 'nation-state'. If the state no longer represents the interests of the nation in the international system of nation-states but comes to represent the interests of global finance to the nation, and if the majority of the nation cannot see in the state an agency that seeks to reconcile with some degree of fairness the competing interests of the various classes and other social forces within the nation, then the very basis and purpose of the nation-state become questionable, especially in a historical situation where energies released by the anti-colonial movement had so very recently endowed the newly independent state with at least a nominal degree of ethical claim. It is in the midst of such stresses of democratic polity and contradictions of historical conjuncture that the need arises to forge, through drastical redefinition, a new kind of nationalist ideology to replace the old one.

That old ideology whose replacement is now sought was of course built around the rational kernel of anti-colonial nationalism, planned and independent economic development, a balance between market exchange and social regulation, popular sovereignty, universal suffrage, the promise of social justice for the oppressed castes, classes, and other subaltern strata, regional autonomy for linguistic nationalities, and secular equality in a multi-denominational society – all the things that have come to be dismissed now, more or less contemptuously, as 'Nehruvian'. It needs to be stressed that the rational kernel summarized above does not describe the actual society that came into being during the premiership of Jawaharlal Nehru – far from it. However, that kernel does signify the utopic horizon that promised to work towards the creation of the conditions of its own realization. The abandoning of that horizon, at once rational and utopic, in a circumstance which continues to require a nationalist ideology, has meant that nationalism itself must now be remade in an irrationalist, fascistic mode: not the Utopia of secular civility and narrowing of inequities but the dystopia of cruelty for oppressed classes and minority communities. Hindutva in the ideological domain, 'liberalization' in domains of public policy, are the two names of that dystopia.

IV

It is sometimes said that Hindutva fascism and economic liberalization are irreconcilable. The argument seems to be based on an analogy with the Nazi regime of the inter-war years. In relation to current Indian politics, moreover, this argument rests on three further propositions: (1) perpetual communal violence is bad for business confidence and those who perpetrate such violence are unlikely candidates for support from Indian big business, multi- national corporations, and imperialist states; (2) since world capitalism is stagnating but not in great crisis, and since working-class militancy is not very vigorous these days, it does not need fascist methods for fighting the working class; and (3) imperialist countries are not likely to view Hindu 'fundamentalism' any more kindly than Muslim 'fundamentalism'. None of these propositions seems quite valid. Imperialism has had much difficulty with Muslim 'fundamentalism' in Iran where it attacked bases for all kinds of American power in and around that country, but no such difficulty with Muslim 'fundamentalism' in Pakistan when it served American interest or in Afghanistan when it fought against the Soviet Union – and of course never in Saudi Arabia, the model fundamentalist state. Even if we grant that Hindutva is 'fundamentalist', which is much to be doubted, its friendliness not only towards 'liberalization' but also towards a whole range of US policies will still win it many friends among Non Resident Indians (NRIs), multi-national corporations, etc. As for violence and business confidence, the Sangh parivar seems not to be committed to perpetual violence of a kind that rocks urban centres, let alone capitalist enterprises, for any length of time. For the most part, it practises perpetual but low-intensity violence, strictly against its communal targets, to undermine the self- confidence of the minorities and to establish Hindutva supremacy among the Hindus with a use of force so judicious that the bourgeoisie has no reason to feel threatened by it. The Bombay riots of 1992, which erupted in the wake of the Ayodhya demonstrations, were an exception rather than the rule, and the reason why neither the state nor the big bourgeoisie nor the dominant media have been much bothered by this violence is that they know how very safe from it they are.[9] Indeed, so far as actual use of violence is concerned, the success of Hindutva is that it has succeeded in making communal violence a normal part of Indian life by giving to this violence a very precise focus; they have also demonstrated in practice that violence does not become more widespread, more unpredictable, more disruptive in the states – the largest states in the Union (Uttar Pradesh, Madhya Pradesh) as well as the nerve centre of Indian capital (Maharashtra) – that they have governed. In the Centre, moreover, they promise a no-nonsense, strong, law-and-order state. As regards the argument that imperialism does not need fascism today because the level of workers' militancy is not very high, the plain fact about the history of the past fifty years is that low levels of working-class militancy have never prevented imperialism from supporting a wide variety of dictatorships and authoritarian regimes of the extreme Right in the majority of Third World countries, not to speak of its support for Zionist racism in Israel and apartheid in South Africa, whatever the level of working-class militancy.

The problem with all such arguments is that they proceed through analogy: since conditions prevailing within India nationally and for capitalism globally in the present decade are structurally different from the ones that prevailed for Germany nationally and in its global environment during the 1930s, it is thereby shown that India cannot repeat the German experience. Which is of course all too true, but such logic still begs the real questions: (1) if the Hindutva offensive signifies a 'Hindu nationalism', as is sometimes argued, then we still have to specify what kind of nationalism it is, considering that fascism has historically risen on the base of ultra-nationalism; and (2) if it is a fascism – in India, at the close of the century – not in the 1930s, not in Europe – then what are the features that are specific to this place and this historical moment, the German experience notwithstanding? It is in relation to this problem of historical and even conjunctural specificity that one needs to enquire why it is, then, that the ideological work and organizational techniques of RSS and other similar organizations, which remained marginal in the political life of India for some fifty years, from the mid-1920s onward, have suddenly begun succeeding over the past twenty – especially the past ten – years. I have argued that it is the lapsing of the Nehruvian, left-of-centre hegemony, coupled with the failure of the Left to provide a national alternative, which has opened the way for this offensive from the Right. This point can be argued in yet another way, through a comparison not with Nazi Germany in the 1930s but with some other states in Asia and Africa during this same period, and through some comparative comments on the rise of Islamicist extremism in the Middle East and North Africa, and Hindutva extremism in India.

India's postwar experience is part and parcel of a global experience, and it is sometimes useful to forgo the idea of Indian exceptionalism and to look at ourselves as a part of the wider world. A couple of aspects of this epochal experience are worthy of note here. To start with, the postwar period of fifty years can be more or less neatly divided into two halves, wherein the first twenty-five years witnessed enormous economic growth globally while the latter twenty-five years, from the mid-1970s onward, have been years of general stagnation (even in the advanced capitalist countries), outright negative growth (as in sub-Saharan Africa), and/or systemic collapse (notably in the erstwhile COMECON countries).[10] These distinct phases of prosperity and decline in the economic domain have had remarkable analogues in domains of ideology and politics as well. Those earlier years of relative prosperity witnessed the triumph of Keynesianism in the advanced capitalist countries in the form of welfarist reformism; expansion of the non-capitalist world to encompass roughly a third of humanity; waves of revolutionary upheavals through much of the backward zones of capital and workers' militancy in parts of southern Europe itself; decolonization across Asia and Africa, articulation of radical nationalism and aspiration for independent development on the part of a number of national bourgeoisies in the Afro-Asian zone: from Indonesia to Ghana, including India and Egypt. By contrast, the next twenty-five years witnessed a general retreat from the welfare state under advanced capitalism; the dismantling of the radical-nationalist state in such countries as Egypt, India, and Algeria;[11] the fall of European communism and restoration of capitalism in the remaining states in Asia (China, Vietnam); a general renunciation of revolutionary and radical hopes in favour of a globalized neo-laissez-faire implemented in the advanced zones by conservative and social democratic regimes alike (Reagan in the United States, Mitterrand in France), and through pressures of the multilateral agencies in the rest of the world – now, increasingly, in India as well.

During this latter period, we have witnessed three key developments in the ideological domain, two of which have been extensively recognized across the globe: the retreat of Marxism, and the triumph of the neo-liberalist ideas of Friedmanite-Hayekian pedigree. What needs greater recognition, however, is the drastic redefinition of nationalism itself, especially in the erstwhile radical-nationalist states, in a quasi-religious, politically irrationalist mode. This is as true of Egypt or Algeria as of India itself. It is on the prior basis of the dashed hopes of the period of Nasser and the FLN that Islamicist extremism has arisen in Egypt and Algeria respectively, to occupy that same space of nationalist aspiration which has been left vacant after the lapsing of the left-of-centre secular nationalisms. In that sense, extremist political Hinduism which arises to prominence in India after the demise of Nehruvian radical nationalism is structurally similar to those Islamicist extremisms of Egypt and Algeria. The difference is that those Islamisms retain, as regards the question of imperialism, an organic relation with projects of the radical nationalist past; most of the Islamicist activists who participated in the assassination of Sadat had been Nasserists in their youth and now hoped that Islamism would achieve for them the anti-imperialist goals that Nasserism promised and didn't deliver. The Islamicist radicals of contemporary Algeria, who have launched such a bloody war against secular society in general, seek nevertheless to recoup the objectives of the anti-colonial revolution in the mould, now, of an austere, punitive, masculinist, scripturalist, and authoritarian Islam.[12] Both of those Islamisms, the Egyptian and the Algerian, are, in the most accurate sense, movements of the radical Right, very much in the image of 'national socialism'. Hindu extremism in India has grown in similar circumstances of the demise of the radical-nationalist state but it seeks, by contrast, not the completion of the anti-colonial project but its repudiation, and seeks not the defeat of imperialism but reconciliation with it and subordination to it. It seeks not to complete the anti-imperialist mission that the Nehruvian state failed to accomplish but to repudiate that mission itself, while what it takes from the legacies of 'national socialism' is the racist content but not the social radicalism: that is why it defines its so-called 'nationalism' not in opposition to the colonial rule of yesterday or the imperialist domination of today but the Muslim imperium of the medieval past. How limited are the capacities of Islamicist anti-imperialism we can learn from the experience of the successful revolution of radical Islam in Iran under Khomeini's austere and brutal leadership, the limits and contours of which foretell the fate of Islamism in Algeria if it were to succeed. The masculinisms and brutalities of Hindu extremism are comparable, but its historic visions and capacities are even more paltry.

A nationalist ideology that can serve as the cement of society is the objective requirement of a nation-state such as the Indian, in a historical moment such as the present. But a culturalist, rightward redefinition of nationalism, stripped of anti-imperialist content but designed for irrationalist mobilization, is also a requirement of this moment of imperialist triumph, when the liberationist imagination released by the Bolshevik Revolution is everywhere in retreat and many kinds of irrationalisms are stalking all the zones of this earth. In this, too, Hindutva fascism is not very original, in the sense that nostalgic and irrationalist populism of the extreme Right is a general tendency around the globe today, in Western Europe as much as in the Middle East and South Asia; together, such movements serve to stabilize the defeat of communism and anti-imperialist nationalism on the global scale, as well as the triumph of imperialism in a moment of capitalist stagnation. In other words, if welfarist reformism was the capitalist solution for the period of prosperity and of offensives from the Left, neo-liberalist economy and irrationalist populism may well be regarded as a general solution for the period of stagnation; and if, within India, Nehruvian social democracy corresponded to the earlier phase, Hindutva is suitable for the latter.

It is in this larger perspective that the ideological construct of Hindutva and the public policy of liberalization are not only reconcilable but complementary. Policies of liberalization can succeed only if Indian nationalism can be detached from its historic anti-colonial origins and redefined in culturalist, irrationalist, racist terms, so that national energies are expanded not on resistance against imperialism but on suppression of the supposed enemy within: the denominational minority, the communist Left, the 'pseudo-secularist', any and all oppositions to 'tradition' as defined by Hindutva and its accomplices among the indigenist sophists. I might add that in this redefinition of nationalism, 'religion' serves in the Islamicist and Hinduizing ideologies much the same function – of exclusion of the other, purification of the self – that 'race' has historically had in the making of imperialist and fascist ideologies in Europe.

If the above proposition is in any fundamental sense true, two further points may be made. First, in our denunciation of what Romila Thapar quite correctly calls 'syndicated Hinduism', on the ground that it is based on a false homogenization of a Hinduism which is by its nature only the sum of diverse, local, mutable traditions, we have not paid enough attention to the fact that the issue of truth and falsity, and our way of posing true Hinduism as against false Hinduism of the RSS, addresses only a part and perhaps a secondary part of the problem. The power of this falsely homogenized Hinduism perhaps lies elsewhere – in the articulation of the growing integration of the Indian market and communicational grids with the invention of a belief system that can be widely shared, easily packaged, reduced to a linear explanatory narrative, ready to serve more or less as a secularized ideology through TV serialization and mass spectacle, to give to the nation a symbolic unity, on the terrain of hysterical religiosity, which compensates for the lack of a progressive national project in the material domain. In other words, it is only a homogenizing Hinduism that can serve as compensation and substitute for secular nationalism as such. In the cultural sphere, the decisive moment within this process of mass syndication perhaps came through the agency of neither the scholar nor the political demagogue but in mass media, through print iconographies and popular cinema where gods and goddesses from diverse devotional practices and textual sources got slotted into a small number of plot outlines, so that multiplicity got reduced to a system of equivalences through the narrative structure itself. Perhaps the real ingenuity of the RSS was that it adopted, at the moment of its own inception and consistently since then, the figure of Ram as the one upon whom all narrative structures converge, so that the later televising of the Ramayana and the Mahabharata in quick succession created a sense of their mutual continuity, the story of Ram overlapping with heroic narratives of the sacred nation, and when Mr Advani's rath yatra got going it was seen as an extension of those epics; hence Advani's audacity in borrowing elements – e.g., the image of Ram as warrior-king, the trishul of Shiva, the charioteering of Krishna – from both the epics in fabricating the symbology of his pseudo-pilgrimage. The immediacy of the TV screen and the infinite repeatability of the celluloid image of course served to compress time into linearity and simultaneity, so that the fictional reenactment of mythic time could be made to flow with great ease into the political exhortation of the present moment. Thus, far from being simply the false representation of a true tradition, this syndicated Hinduism is remarkably true not to its purported origins in 'Tradition' but to its fabrication in front of our own eyes, almost literally, in the form of political spectacles, much aided by technologies of film and television, for mass consumption by all those who participate in an integrated national market of commodities and ideologies alike, for purposes of a consumerist, market-oriented nationalism as opposed to an anti-imperialist one.

If communalism for the RSS is really only the cutting edge for the popularization of a fascist national project – which gains its strength both from selectively incorporating and elaborating elements of antecedent reform movements and nationalist articulations, and which came about to challenge and displace the Centre-Left power blocs that had previously contended for hegemony – then it necessarily follows that the posing of secularism against communalism is necessary but insufficient; that the posing of the more humane and subversive traditions within the belief systems of the Indian past against the Sangh's masculinist and market-friendly Hinduism is necessary but insufficient; and that it is not possible in fact to challenge a fully articulated fascist national project without posing against it a superior national project capable of organizing what Gramsci once called the 'national-popular will'. To the extent that it is on the terrain of tradition and culture, community and nation, that the fascist project sets out to assemble popular consent for a conservative compact on issues of class and gender, caste and denominational diversity, centralized power and regional autonomy, one cannot abandon the terrain of nationalism itself, and all that that implies for issues of culture and community, tradition and modernity; but one cannot occupy that terrain empty-handed, without a political project for the remaking of the nation and its existing structures of power.

The aim of all cultural politics is the making of a different political culture, and before setting out to reorganize the field of Indian culture, the RSS had set out to establish itself organizationally as an alternative claimant to state power. It is this condensation of the issue of culture as the issue of state power – that is to say, the problem of taking hold of national culture through an organized political force – that the Left, in all its dispersals and molecular movements, has eventually to address as a collective entity. And, I do mean 'collective entity'. Aside from the enormous financial resources at its command, which the Left by its very nature can never match, the main strategic strength of the RSS is its organizational capacity simultaneously to disperse its personnel into numerous forms of activity in all walks of national life and, at strategic moments, to concentrate diverse types of personnel for particular mobilizations and spectacles. The spectacle that they organized around the destruction of the Babri Masjid was a high point following upon some years of this momentum of alternate dispersals and concentrations, virtually military in its precision and siege-like quality – alternating between rapid movement and war of position, as it were. For the Left – all of it, 'organized' and 'unorganized' – there are lessons in the elaboration of that painstaking work, and there is reason to reexamine the very mode of anti-fascist mobilizations during these same years, which have been essentially local and dispersed, even mutually discrete, with none of the advantages of initiative that moments of concentration bring.

V

For some sixty years now, the RSS has followed a two-pronged strategy: (1) the building of a hard core of cadres specializing in different kinds of tasks, and (2) the propagation of its ideas in the culture at large through highly innovative means. Over forty years ago, it added the crucial third prong to its strategy, namely the formation of distinct but overlapping mass fronts, the number of which have increased. To the extent that it chose the mercantile bourgeoisie as its principal collaborator and source of finance, and to the extent that it has always treated the urban petty bourgeoisie as the strategic class in the making of insurgencies in modern societies, it has historically devoted less energy and finance to its class fronts among peasants and workers, especially peasants, and has concentrated on four types of fronts: (1) the front of students and intellectuals, (2) the fronts that help it cement ties with the traditional sectors for religious legitimation, (3) the fronts which connect it with the urban lumpen elements, and (4) the crucial parliamentary front. It is through these fronts, and by grooming college students as the bureaucrats and professionals of tomorrow, that it has gained its influence in the media and the state apparatuses, from top to bottom, without taking power. These, then, have been the main elements of the power bloc: mercantile capital, intellectuals and other professional petty bourgeois, the milling crowds on the margins of the modern sector, the urban lumpens – and, to the extent that our modes of urbanization tend to lumpenize large segments of the working class, the lumpenized workers as well. Almost the most striking feature of the recent expansion of the RSS and some of its fronts into the countryside is their ability to make flexible, caste-specific, region-specific alliance with sections of the upwardly mobile middle caste peasantries and the growing rural bourgeoisie in the agrarian economy. Considering that it set out to challenge the formidable political hegemony of Congress nationalism, in the face of grand figures like Gandhi and Nehru, it has displayed remarkable endurance, almost Gramscian in its will, to defend its key positions by digging deep trenches. In the process, it has sought to address, from the position of the extreme Right, some organizational questions regarding techniques of insurrection, of the kind on which so much of the Left movement in Europe, Latin America, and India has historically come to grief: (1) the problem of resolving the dichotomy between cadre party and mass party; (2) the problem of organizing parliamentary and non-parliamentary work simultaneously; (3) the problem of organizing an insurgent movement within the parliamentary Republic of the bourgeoisie by making use of the openness of the democratic system and combining that legal work with cadre-based, extra-legal assaults; (4) the problem of keeping nationwide social networks available within the interstices of democratic society for the cadre party to retreat into if and when the weight of state power comes down heavily, without damaging the work of mass fronts and parties; and (5) the problem of avoiding a frontal confrontation with the repressive apparatus of the democratic state and yet gradually forcing the internal erosion of both the repressive and the chief political apparatuses of the constituted state, until state power is ready, like a ripened fruit, for seizure. Fundamentally, it has had to face a historically unique problem: the organization of a movement inspired by historic forms of fascism but in a society marked both by backward capitalism, unlike Germany, and, unlike Italy or Spain, by powerful traditions of electoral democracy based on universal franchise in a context of entrenched civil and military bureaucracies largely subservient to secular political authority.

That the RSS has been truly in command of its fronts, despite their enormous size and resources, is quite evident from the fact that at no point in its history has the RSS depended on its parliamentary front for its own expansion. It did not even have such a front until after it was banned in the aftermath of Gandhi's assassination, even though it is said to have acquired upward of 100,000 cadres and active participants by the beginning of the Second World War and perhaps as many as 700,000 by 1948.[13] At no point was there any correspondence between the electoral fortunes of the Jana Sangh, the first parliamentary front and the precursor of BJP, and the rate of growth of the RSS. The slow pace of its growth between 1948 and 1962 is fully explainable in terms of the widespread perception of its complicity in Gandhi's assassination and the national power of Nehruvianism on the one hand, that of the united CPI on the other. By contrast, the contraction of parliamentary seats from

93 for Jan Sangh in 1977 to merely 2 for BJP in 1984 was accompanied by the doubling of RSS shakhas during those same years.[14] What I am suggesting is that the electoral arithmetic is subject to so many other factors that there is no necessary correspondence between the fortunes of the parliamentary front and the cultural logic or organizational design pursued by the RSS itself. It is perfectly possible, in an extreme case, that the BJP declines definitively as an electoral force while the RSS goes from strength to strength as much in cadre-building as in the building of a national cultural consensus so that countless individuals who vote for other parties actually come to adopt the whole of the RSS world-view, while electoral encashment of the sea-change in the cultural life of the nation takes place much later.

This does not imply that the electoral process does not fundamentally matter. It matters in all sorts of ways: in terms of specific political parties gaining access to enormous material resources and social authority; as legitimation through what one may call the mass psychology of liberal democracy as to who is authorized to rule; and as the central mechanism in the processes for negotiating and renegotiating the intricacies of the social compact. The more unruly the ruling class becomes, the more one needs the integrity of this process to protect what democratic culture and public civility there is. What I mean is quite else. First, the Left parties on the one hand, the RSS and allied forces on the other, are the only ones that represent specific kinds of political culture, and that to the extent that the Left parties are restricted largely to their regional bases, the culture at large is wide open for imperceptible but cumulative shifts towards the positions of the Sangh, perhaps not on specific issues but in their generality. Second, the political discourse of the Sangh has a ring of familiarity in a culture replete with authoritarian forms of religiosity, and every failure to build the new in ways vigorous enough to allow large masses of people to take the risk of novelty must always push large sections of those people to seek refuge in what seems familiar; conservatism is born not only from privilege and the will to protect that privilege, but also from the experience of pain and the fear of future pain. Third, the political imaginary that the RSS propagates is based squarely on the near-universal misery of the proletarianized mass and the lower petty bourgeoisie in our cities, which makes them prone to millenarian ideologies, fascist mobilizations, and cultures of cruelty, by invoking images of a vast community that purportedly offers the securities of a parivar in a world where such solidarities are eroded and collapsing, and by invoking hallucinations of power in the midst of powerlessness, real and vast. Because these injuries and the compensatory hallucinations are the fate of the majority of the population, parliamentary democracy itself, with its universal franchise, can be made to serve, to an extent, the fascist purpose.

Such are some of the strengths of the RSS, its fronts, its allied forces. Is their success inevitable? The only possible answer is that we do not yet know; that the future is still wide open; that the outcome of their offensive will depend as much on their own strategic abilities as on (1) the capacity of the centrist forces to stem their own ongoing fragmentation and hold the line on liberal values, and (2) the capacity of the dispersed anti-fascist forces to build an anti-fascist movement. The virulence of the communalist offensive should not be allowed, in any case, to obscure the fact that the factors and forces that are ranged against Hindutva in India today are formidable – commanding, among other things, an absolute numerical majority.

It is also eminently arguable that the real gravitational pull in Indian political culture, as regards religion, is still towards a tolerant multi-denominationality and heterogeneity of belief systems, despite the homogenizing thrusts of Hindutva, the market economy, and the attendant communication systems. And we shall shortly comment on some key weaknesses of the parivar, notably its lack of populist radicalism in the socio-economic domain. However, one also encounters a rather different argument – and one which I would view with some scepticism – to the effect that the balance, indeed the very structure, of class forces in contemporary India precludes the possibility of a fascist resolution. In this context, we may briefly recall some aspects of Italian Fascism which should be of particular interest to us, considering that unlike Nazi Germany, which was the most industrialized country in Europe at the time, the Italy of Mussolini's day was relatively much less industrialized and predominantly agrarian.[15]

The experience of Italy, the classic home of Fascism, shows that Fascism can come to power easily and rule confidently in semi- industrialized countries of backward capital, even though the majority of the population may be agrarian and largely illiterate. Indeed, the success of Fascism in key rural regions such as the Po Valley was crucial in its emergence as a national force. It shows also that neither finance capital nor the big bourgeoisie in general actually created Fascism but then acquiesced in its power, once established, when it became clear that no stable centrist force was available for the management of capitalist accumulation; only towards the end of 1920, well after the spread of Fascist squads in large parts of Italy and less than a year before Mussolini's rise to power, did the big magnates of industry and commerce begin even to finance him, while his initial appointment as Prime Minister, at the head of a minority government, came with the consent not only of the army but also of the historic liberal bloc. The Italian experience also shows that in a semi-industrialized country the principal class forces of Fascism are comprised of mercantile capital (the Milanese merchants were the first sizeable bloc of the urban rich to go over to Fascism), the professional petty bourgeoisie, the educated unemployed (i.e., the potential professional stratum that feels frustrated by low levels of accumulation, few job opportunities, and eschewed distribution of wealth), the lumpenized mass, those landowners who are directly besieged by the peasantry; big capital, on any substantial scale, is the last to join. The fact that the big bourgeoisie neither created Fascism nor played any significant role in its capture or consolidation of power meant that the Mussolini regime remained relatively autonomous of that bourgeoisie even after it made common cause with it. A significant consequence was that after he had smashed the Communist and Socialist trade unions, as the bourgeoisie had desired, he dictated to the bourgeoisie that his party was to have the sole right to form unions; in turn, Fascist monopoly over the unions, which made it impossible for workers to represent themselves in collective bargaining through other means, meant that considerable sections of the working class began then to cooperate with Fascist rule.

In the ideological domain, four aspects of Italian Fascism are striking. First, Mussolini had been an illustrious member of the Socialist Party and continued to speak, even as a Fascist, in a populist language of promising higher standards of living for the poor through brisk national development; his was a radicalism of the Right but a radicalism nevertheless, which he abandoned to a very large extent but only after taking power.

Second, he at once invoked that nationalism which had fought for Italian independence some fifty years earlier and criticized it for not having accomplished enough for the nation, thus presenting Fascism as a re-invigorated ultra-nationalism necessary to correct the wrongs of the misguided nationalism of the previous liberal regimes. Third, anti-communism was woven into the rhetoric of this ultra-nationalism. And finally, Mussolini constantly invoked the classical and

imperial traditions of Rome in holding out the promise that the authoritarian, strong nation-state that he was building was necessary for reviving the nation's tradition and glory. In this invocation of 'Tradition', religion played a paradoxical role. In the initial phase of the Fascist offensive against the organized Left and the labour movement, Fascism collided also with the populist religion and agrarian radicalism of the Catholic peasant leagues which were opposed to both Socialism and Fascism at that stage. However, as Mussolini moved to consolidate his power with the help of the liberals themselves, and especially as he aligned himself with the Catholic Church and received the Pope's blessing, the public anti-Fascism of the 'good' Catholics collapsed. Thereafter, the political power of organized Catholicism became a fundamental component of the Fascist regime without Italy becoming in any way a theocratic state. This is useful to recall in the present Indian context, in the sense that hysterical kinds of irrationalist religiosity – more broadly speaking, religious legitimation as such – does not become any the less important in the fascistic mobilizations of Hindutva just because the RSS and its allies do not wish to turn India formally into a theocracy.

So far as the relation between the bourgeoisie and fascist politics is concerned, we might say that the point of unity for the capitalist class is capital itself, and what the whole class always wants is a political authority that would ensure stable conditions for the expanded reproduction of capital. Otherwise, in its conditions of normal political existence, the class is comprised of competing enterprises, groups, and fractions, clustering around different contenders for state power. What happens typically is that some units of capital throw in their support for fascism early on, but it is usually in the process of fascism's coming to power that more and more units of capital begin to cluster around it; fascism's rise has to take on the appearance of inevitability before competing units of capital suspend their political squabbles and unite behind the rising power. This corresponds to the Marxist postulate of a certain formal separation, in the capitalist mode of production, between (to use Engels's terminology) the 'governing caste' and the 'ruling class' and the relative (only relative) autonomy of the political from the economic. We might add that because fascism comes to power with the force of a mass movement of the radical Right, with formidable bases among the mercantile and the petty bourgeoisies, its autonomy in relation to the 'coupon-clippers' (Lenin's phrase for finance capital) is, in relative terms, even greater than is normal for parliamentary regimes of the bourgeoisie.

In every country where fascism has come to power or even close to power, the crucial elements have been: the size of the army of the unemployed (including the educated unemployed) and the misery of the working classes; the fear and disaffection of the petty bourgeoisie caught between economic disintegration and inflation rates; an acute sense of real or imagined national injuries in the present, combined with a virtually pathological belief in past glories of race, nation, religious community; the existence of social minorities and political radicals that are portrayed as the real culprits in economic decay and national injury; growth of militancy among the immiserated; a collapsing liberal Centre that contrasts sharply with the aggressive and disciplined character of the fascist party. It is the ripening of this conjuncture which eventually tends to press the big bourgeoisie finally to make up its mind in fascism's favour.

That substantial elements of this conjuncture exist in India accounts for the growth of the fascist tendency here, and even the lack of working-class militancy is partially compensated for by the existence of large Communist Parties, the always local but nationwide activities of the anti-communal forces (which are objectively anti-fascist even where their immediate impulse is simply liberal and humanitarian), and the renewed assertion of dalits and Other Backward Castes (OBCs), which is a form of class struggle even though the inability of the Left to provide progressive leadership for them opens up the space for opportunists, demagogues, and even criminal elements to fill the vacuum of organization and leadership.

VI

The principal problem for the RSS, in this regard, is not that it lacks the support of the big bourgeoisie but that (1) it is operating in a society far more heterogenous than any where fascism has succeeded in the past; (2) it lacks that class radicalism of the classic fascist parties which could offer to the immiserated something more substantial than the intoxicants of religious ideology and fascist spectacle; and (3) the centrist forces – from the Congress to the Janata Dal (JD) – are already agreed on the destruction of the progressive aspects of the Indian state and its economic policies so that the RSS is unable to offer to foreign monopolies and Indian corporate capital a substantially more attractive economic package. Hence its concentration on symbolic politics and its floundering on the substantive issues. It posits the Mandir issue against Mandal – i.e., an essentially brahminical project against the upsurge of the dominated castes – but then sets out to co-opt the OBCs when the electoral arithmetic so requires. It has a far-reaching alliance with Shiv Sena in both the parliamentary and non-parliamentary domains but then recoils from Sena's rampaging against dalits in order to conceal its own overwhelmingly upper-caste character, and to placate the more populist elements in its own ranks. BJP, the parliamentary front of the RSS, sets out to be the party of saffron yuppies but then other fronts of the RSS start opposing, at least formally, part of the BJP's own neo-liberal agenda so as to appeal to the nascent nationalism of the larger sections of the Indian intelligentsia. The RSS supports the most murderously militarist solutions in Punjab but then turns around to placate the Sikhs in Delhi in the course of its own confrontation with the Congress in the city. It presents itself as the party of Hindu purity and rectitude but spawns a parliamentary front, namely the BJP itself, that becomes increasingly indistinguishable from the Congress as regards corruption, factionalism, and power play of all kinds.

The contradictions of these policies ought not to be seen simply as incoherence, since it is the classic ambition of fascist parties to be all things to all people. Yet it is also the case that the immense heterogeneities of Indian society are such that an onward march of a unified fascist force is very difficult in the light of contrary pulls in all the arenas of caste, region, class, community, and faction. The kind of problem the RSS faces owing to its own lack of class radicalism even of a rightwing kind becomes clear if we compare its trajectory to the one situation where a religio-clerical elite, arising in a society which had as much civilizational depth as India itself, did organize a mass movement-based primarily on religious legitimation, mercantile capital, the urban petty bourgeoisie, the proletarianized mass, even substantial sections of the working class – for an insurrectionary seizure of power. I mean, Khomeini'ite Iran! I do not offer any exact parallels here, because situations are always concrete and drawing false parallels is usually very dangerous, but some discrete contrasts may help us comprehend at least some of our own unique specificity.[16]

Unlike the Khomeini'ite religio-clerical forces, which organized their power bloc against a monarchical system commanding no institutions of popular legitimation and where the essential structure of power was concentrated in the hands of a monarcho-bourgeoisie comprised of not much more than two thousand households, the RSS and its allies face in India institutions of the parliamentary republic where power is too widely distributed, with a vibrant civil society, comprised, in Gramsci's vivid phrase, of ramparts and trenches so numerous as to be unavailable for quick dismantling through frontal assault or a war of rapid movement. Unlike Athna-'Ashari Shi'ism of Iran, which has no parallel in histories of Sunni Islam and which is as hierarchically structured as medieval Catholicism, the RSS seeks religious legitimation from belief systems which have neither institutional homogeneity nor a unified clergy. When one says that 90 per cent of the Irani population subscribes actively to the 'Athna-'Ashari branch of Shi'ism, one means that, as of 1978, the year of the Irani Revolution, the entire elaborate network of mosques and medrissas was run by a grand total of less than half a million individuals directly organized in a strictly hierarchical pyramid controlled, at the top, by no more than about a dozen ayatollahs and Marajai-e-taqlid. To say, by contrast, that over 80 per cent of India constitutes a majority community bound by a single religious system called Hinduism is, strictly speaking, nonsensical. Not only are divisions of caste and sect and math, of sense and sensibility and belief itself, in local and regional variations, far too numerous, but what we provisionally call Hinduism also has no institutional analogue for the Irani kind of religious pyramid, not even remotely, no matter how many mahants and sadhvis RSS collects under its banner, and no matter how many Shankaracharyas wax eloquent in support of religious obscurantism – nor can that kind of homogenization be produced instantly, through modern means of communication and organization of spectacles, because technological fabrication also has its limits. The Shankaracharyas themselves have no institutionalized authority even remotely resembling the authority of the Irani Marajai-e-taqlid.

But my next point is the more crucial one, namely that the fundamental weakness of the RSS and its fronts is that they are formations of a conservative Right, not of a radical Right. Ali Shariati's version of Islam was somewhat more radical than the radical nationalism of Frantz Fanon; the programme of redistributive justice advocated by Ayatollah Taleghani was no less radical than that of the Tudeh, the historic Communist Party of Iran – and Taleghani was the Ayatollah of Teheran, with the right to use the radio and television on at least each Friday. Taleghani, I might add, commanded a very substantial following in those sections of the Teherani middle class that supported the Irani Revolution – and, so radical was his vision of post-revolutionary Iran that when Khomeini returned from Paris, Taleghani did not even go forward to greet him, because he knew that Khomeini was a man ultimately of the authoritarian Right, even though Khomeini's hatred of American subjugation of Iran was second to none and even though Khomeini intended to nationalize the properties of the monarcho-bourgeoisie, and indeed did so. That monarcho-bourgeoisie ran from his Iran as rapidly as the Tsarist aristocracy had run from Lenin's Russia. In the process, the Irani Revolution redefined for radical Islam a familiar word: mustazafin, which came to be the Farsi equivalent for Frantz Fanon's term 'wretched of the earth.'

I am no admirer of the Irani Revolution. Rather, I have used the term 'clerico-fascist' for the regime that ensued from Khomeini's takeover. That, however, is another story. The point I am making here is that the religious idiom that was deployed to build immense resources of political hegemony in Iran addressed issues not just of religious identity but of the monarchical institution, the expropriation of the big bourgeoisie, freedom from foreign economic and military domination, welfare guarantees for the mustazafin, strict controls over the vulgarities of conspicuous consumption, radical revisions of property relations. Its economic programme was remarkably similar to the entirely secular programme of Nasserism in Egypt or the original programme of the Algerian FLN as expounded in the Tripoli Declaration before Independence.

What I am suggesting is that the RSS – along with its fronts and affiliates – has a national project for the unmaking and remaking of India in its own image. They take advantage of the misery of the majority of the Indian peoples; they build, simultaneously, on the reservoirs of mass resentment and the fatalistic notion of conservative religiosity that all shall be well if homogenized pieties can be imposed upon our personal, social, political lives; and on the notion, made familiar by the Nazis, that the misery of the body politic can be blamed entirely on the socio-religious minority, and that periodic pogroms of that minority and the bellicosities of majoritarian ultra-nationalism can help postpone forever the issue of resolving the material bases of that misery. They raise, in other words, the issue of mass misery only to suppress and wilfully misrecognize the sources of that misery.

VII

The issue of secularism surfaces in discussions of the sources and possible remedies of Indian misery in peculiar ways. From the RSS to our indigenist social scientists, not to speak of many avantgarde historians, all sorts of people are agreed that the kind of hard secularism that appeals to no religious tradition and seeks to justify itself in terms of its own logic is not suitable for us because of its Western origin and its supposed incompatibility with our traditions.[17] This, I must confess, is peculiar. After all, the same people do use much that originated initially in Europe: railways, aeroplanes, a whole range of Euro-American ideas from the most mundane and conservative to the most fashionably postmodern.[18] The point, I should have thought, was usefulness, and the secular form of politics should get at least the same hearing as railways or computers, with reference not to origins but purposes. Since European origin is the issue, however, it might be best to recall a particular history, so as to clarify that while certain historical forms have indeed been radically different, the problems of denominational and sectarian strife that the transition from theocracy and religious legitimation to secular governance in histories of early modern Europe sought to address are analogous to the problems we ourselves have had to face in the course of the formation of modern, sovereign, democratic states in South Asia and the Middle East.

The historical process that eventually gave rise to fully fledged secularisms in the recent history of Europe, in the sense of a juridical separation between political life and religious life, actually began much earlier, with those crises of the sixteenth century which then witnessed, on the one hand, the rise of a number of centralized states in monarchical and bureaucratic forms; and, on the other, the catastrophic wars of the Reformation and Counter-Reformation, which had the cumulative effect of dividing Europe along religious lines, Catholic and Protestant, and of endowing each large state with religious minorities and dissenting sects: Protestants in Catholic France, Catholics in Anglican Britain, Jewish minorities in overwhelmingly Christian countries, and so on. The idea of a separation between religion and politics, which is internally essential for the emergence of a modern civil society based on equal citizenship, was posed as a secularist compact, first of all, to obtain the peace between neighbouring states founded on prior histories of religious conflict; second, to obtain a modicum of safety for the religious minorities, dissidents, and smaller sects – as Protestantism itself had given rise to many different churches along lines of doctrinal difference; and, third, to gain for the newly constituted centralized states a modicum of freedom from the Vatican even inside the world of Catholicism. The issue of minorities – all kinds of minorities – was thus central in establishing the link between the idea of secularity and the idea of citizenship (or at least subject status) in territorially defined states. Recent researches suggest that what later flowered into the High Enlightenment, centred in France, perhaps had its intellectual origins in a number of currents that arose initially out of the English Revolution of the mid-seventeenth century, ranging from the more moderate Newtonian Enlightenment to those heterodoxies, dissents, and even pantheisms for which anti-clerical ideas were deeply tied to republican anti-monarchism.[19] The movement for the separation of religion and state was irrevocably a part, in other words, of the project for the democratization of the latter. Prominent among the exponents of such ideas seem to have been the remarkably mobile mass of religious refugees and dissenters: those who had fled from the Restoration in Britain after Cromwell; those who had organized dissents within their own churches and were therefore persecuted or driven away; and Jews fleeing from Christianity, Protestants from Catholicism, Catholics from Protestantism, Freethinkers from organized religion, etc. Many of them congregated in Amsterdam and more particularly The Hague; many of their ideas then travelled to Paris, where some of the Encyclopaedists adopted some of those ideas, mostly in watered-down versions. Traces of those origins are there in genealogies of British liberalism as well, from Locke to John Stuart Mill, where a moderate discourse that began by attempting to reconcile the democratic demand for popular rights with constitutional monarchy proceeded, over time, to pose the idea of individual liberty against the autocracy of the majority. Lockean ideas were of course deeply marked by the ideology of natural rights wherein the individual is the sovereign subject of his own fundamental rights since these rights are his by nature and thus, in a sense, prior to society; Mill, a century or so later, is able to think of the dilemmas of democracy in terms of the minority of one because the central problem of democracy for him is not majority rule but minority rights, and the attendant problem, therefore, of ensuring both the majority's right to rule and the minority's right not only to protection but also to liberty. Hence, the classic question of liberal individualism: does the minority have equal rights and equal liberty even if it is a minority consisting of only one individual?[20]

This type of political liberalism could of course as easily become fully secular and anti-monarchical, in the Constitution of the United States for example, as it could become accommodated to not only the constitutional monarchy in Britain but also to a form in which the monarch is also formally the head of the Church of England. In other words, the British liberalism that arose in the aftermath of regicide and Restoration was democratic enough greatly to restrict the prerogatives of monarchy but also conservative enough to retain a formal tie between church and state. In France, by contrast, where the victory of the Counter-Reformation had been unable wholly to eradicate or even to tame the energies released by forces of the Reformation, anti-clericalism gestated in highly radical forms and when the revolutionary upheaval came towards the end of the eighteenth century it was endowed with a much more sweepingly secular philosophical foundation which transformed the ideas of sovereignty, citizenship, rights, and political subjecthood far more fundamentally.

Absolutism had utilized the idea of the divine right of kingship to make sovereignty an attribute of 'eminence' and to define freedoms as restricted and hierarchically structured in accordance with the ties of dependence and subjection under the highest degree of eminence, namely the monarch as Sovereign. In contrast, the secularizing discourse of the 'Rights of Man and Citizen' inaugurated by 1789 redefines sovereignty as an attribute not of divinely ordained eminence but of collectivity, equality, freedom, and citizenship.[21] In that discourse, sovereignty is of course no longer the (divine or profane) right of kings; but sovereignty is also not understood here as the attribute of each of the individuals separately, in such a way that they merely pool together their separate freedoms in order to constitute a collective sovereignty through aggregation of individual wills. In other words, this discourse of course denies that rights are given by either a divinity or by 'nature'; however, contrary to many misunderstandings, it also does not constitute the individual as the sovereign subject of rights in political society. Rather, sovereignty in this discourse is from the start an attribute of free and equal citizens in their collectivity. The individual comes to have an inalienable share in the prerogatives of sovereignty not by virtue of a natural right but by virtue of belonging already in civil society as a subject of civil law, and in political society (the state) as citizen; to the extent that the distinction between civil society and the state is essentially a methodological one, the relatedness of these two forms of belonging may be summarized in the hyphenated term, Subject-Citizen or Citizen-Subject, depending on which sense of the word 'subject' we wish to foreground. Thus it is that sovereignty in this discourse is fundamentally indivisible and can be exercised only collectively, not individually.[22]

It is in fact the thought of Rousseau that haunts the moment of 1789. He was of course banned by the Church, but he also radically denies that the 'state of nature' is a domain of rights.[23] He posits, rather, a prior location within society and a certain distance from the natural state ('denatured' is Rousseau's own word in this context) for one to have rights of citizenship. The point of origin for rights, in other words, is neither God nor nature but society itself, or what Rousseau called 'the social contract'. However, what Rousseau calls 'the social contract' is not something 'real', a product of an agreement among humans living in a state of nature and deciding to found a civil society; nor is it a moment within temporal history, with a before and an after; the moment of the 'social contract' is not a historically concrete but a philosophically abstract moment, a point zero, which presumes not a negotiated but a common origin, prior to and beyond the realm of individual wills, a point of entry into history already marked by boundedness of civil obligation and social right; Rousseau's 'social contract', unlike Locke's, designates the idea that there is no humanity before society and that society needs no divine sanction to constitute itself. He was deeply suspicious of founding the discourse of rights in the discourse of individuality, prior to society. In an extraordinary aside, Rousseau asserts that he who has individual and unsocial interests can never be a citizen and can only be a bourgeois.

It is from Rousseau's thought, then, that we can trace the productive tension between the conception of citizenship and subjecthood. Historically, the word 'Subject' had carried the predominant meaning of being subjected to the power of the prince, the priest, the patriarch. Princely power implied monarchy; priestly power certainly meant dispensation of souls but it also meant special access to knowledge, through Latin and through a monopoly over schooling, very much as brahminism in India historically implied the debarring of women and shudras from Sanskrit language, and hence Vedic knowledge. While patriarchal power certainly meant serfdom of one sort or another in the realm of agrarian production, it also meant the subjection of women in that realm as well as within the household. What got transformed, in the course of the political upheavals of the eighteenth century and in the thought of the Enlightenment, was even the linguistic meaning of the word 'Subject'.

The discourse of 1789 may be credited with the revolutionary revisions of the meaning of subjecthood, whereby the idea of popular and indivisible sovereignty is born as a practical political project, so that the socialized individual is reborn as citizen and becomes a subject not to the prince or the priest, but of history, exercising the liberty of belief in matters of faith, demanding from the state a system of public and secular education, and instead of obeying the given laws actually participating in the social act of making the laws whereby state and society are to function. As we know, this battle was not won once and for all even in France, and it has had to be fought over and over again, in many corners of the globe. For Rousseau, in any case, true citizenship becomes thinkable only as the ability of the citizens, in their collectivity, to give laws unto themselves but also, equally, in their collective consent to abide by the laws they had given to themselves. The citizen, thus, was both a subject of and subject to: at once the author of laws and the voluntary object of laws, thereby the maker of history but also made by history. It was on the terrain of this doubleness – of being subjected to the laws that one had made as the subject of law – that the conflicting demands of individuality and community were to be reconciled; the community was to be not the community of local origin or otherworldly faith, but the community of equal citizenship that was freely chosen by citizens already bounded in society, and to which, then, one surrendered a part of one's self-interest. I believe that this is the moment in Rousseau's thought which is also, in the history of political philosophy, the point at which the idea of equality, which had started evolving with the issue of secularity within religious society, begins to transform itself into the idea of democracy in the sense in which one would now wish to use this term.

But the truly revolutionary step that Rousseau takes is the second one, in which he asks whether or not citizens who make laws and obey those laws, can in fact be equal subjects of the law, as makers of and as made by the laws, if the distribution of material goods among them is unequal. In other words: is property reconcilable with democracy?[24] Rousseau's thought on this score is both brilliant and faltering, but what I want to suggest through this brief review is that the seeds of democracy are already there in the idea of secularism, because you cannot have popular sovereignty if the state represents a religious majority at the expense of the rights and liberties of a minority; but the idea of socialism is also already there in the idea of democracy because, as Rousseau put it, citizens who are unequal in the property relation cannot be equals, subjects of and as subjects to the law. The Citizen-Subject – that is to say, the democratic individual – cannot be born without the abolition of private property. Rousseau did not quite resolve the problem, even on the level of thought,[25] but in pointing to the incompatibility between property and equality he introduced an irreparable fissure within the body of Enlightenment thought. For, if the conformist strands of the Enlightenment had jubilantly appointed the bourgeois male individual as the rational subject of meaning and experience, strands in the revolutionary politics of the Enlightenment were already pronouncing the impossibility of the birth of the Citizen-Subject in a class-divided society. Hence the watchwords of 1789: 'Liberty, Fraternity, Equality' – which could be translated for our own time, word for word, as 'Democracy, Secularism, Socialism'. It was this particular strand in the politics of the Enlightenment that Marxism picked up, giving to it politically and theoretically a vastly revolutionized meaning, and thereby earning the rebuke of poststructuralists and subalternists alike, to the effect that we are mere children of the Enlightenment. All I can say in response is that, yes, you are damned right, we are – but not merely; not of the whole of the Enlightenment; and not of the Enlightenment only. We are also the spectre that is going to haunt this land for a long, long time.

Let us, then, summarize: the idea of religious liberty and of the peaceful coexistence of religious difference has been central, historically speaking, in the formation of the twin ideas of liberty and equality as such; the idea of democratic dissent was posed initially as the idea of religious difference. It gradually became the premise for the liberties of the individual in general, but then, in this same sweep, raised the difficult question as to how individual rights were to be reconciled with the common good. In raising the question of equality and equal rights for all, the idea of secularism became the chief motor behind the subsequent idea of political democracy. Democracy, in other words, presumes a secularist compact, and it is not liberal democracy that produces the secularist idea; it is the issue of secularism – not just religious tolerance but the civil equality of denominationally different individuals and communities within a given society – that produces the idea of equality in general, and therefore the idea of political democracy.

Democracy, in other words, presumes a prior social consensus on the issue of secular sociality and secular governance. But, what is also implicit in my argument is that the idea of one kind of equality leads, necessarily and logically, to other ideas of equality: the idea of secularism leads to ideas of political democracy, the idea of political equality leads to the idea of economic equality; the idea of socio-economic equality among men leads to similar ideas about equality between men and women, between individuals of one caste and another, one race or nation and another. I do not mean that these ideational logics bring about changes in the material world automatically; the relations between ideas and the material world are always modulated by the dialectic of given structures and transforming human agencies. What I do mean is that ideas of equality in one domain lead necessarily to ideas of equality in other domains; that the logic of such ideas would take us – and should take us – far beyond the conventional confines of democracy or socialism or secularism; that the logic of secularism, the logic of democracy would take us, step by step, to communism itself – in other words, to that utopic moment which is the only realistic resolution of conflicts once the issue of justice has been posed. Because, as I said earlier, once the question of radical equality has been posed, nothing can escape the Utopian ends of that questioning.

Notes

1 This essay was written initially for the workshop on 'Culture, Community, and Nation' organized by the Deccan Development Society on 6-9 December 1993 in Hyderabad, to commemorate the first anniversary of the destruction of the Ayodhya mosque. The brief given to me by the organizers of the Hyderabad workshop was that I should attempt to 'synthesize ... the key issues

that the workshop seeks to address'. I doubt that any one paper can offer such a synthesis, but a point of sharp focus was already implicit in the choice of dates for the workshop itself, for these dates impel us to think of the categories of Culture, Community, and Nation not abstractly but with some specific reference to the destruction of Babri Masjid a year ago, on 6 December 1992, and what that destruction has now come to mean in the life of the body politic. Revised versions and new sections were developed later for talks at SNDT Women's University in Bombay, University of Poona in Pune, and Miranda House in Delhi. Here I extend, with specific reference to contemporary India, the argument I began formulating, more obliquely, in 'Fascism and National Culture: Reading Gramsci in the days of Hindutva'.

2 Prabhat Patnaik and Sumit Sarkar were among those who spoke of fascism in that context. See Prabhat Patnaik, 'The Fascism of Our Times', *Social Scientist* (March-April 1993), 238-9, and Sumit Sarkar, The Fascism of the Sangh Parivar', *Economic and Political Weekly*, 28 (30 January 1993). S. Sarkar seems to have partially distanced himself from that position. See his 'The Anti-Secularist Critique of Hindutva: Problems of a Shared Discursive Space', in *Germinal*, 1 (1994), p. 108, footnote 2.

3 This lecture is reprinted as chapter 5 in my *Lineages of the Present: Political Essays* (London, Verso, 2000).

4 The Sangh parivar is also discussed in chapters 7 and 8 ibid.

5 For a brief summation of these mobilizations, see K.N. Panikkar, 'Religious Symbols and Political Mobilization: The Agitation for a Mandir in Ayodhya', *Social Scientist*, 242-3 (July-August 1993).

6 Articles and even book-length studies on the RSS, its affiliates, activities, and allies – and on communalism in general – are too numerous for quick citation. Few, however, attempt a rounded account of the entire period of this cancerous growth. Among such general narratives, two might be mentioned. A succinct and politically reliable account is to be found in Tapan Basu, Pradip Datta, Sumit Sarkar, Tanika Sarkar, and Sambuddha Sen, *Khaki Shorts, Saffron Flags*, Tracts for the Times/1 (Delhi, Orient Longman, 1993). Walter K. Andersen and Shridhar D. Damle, *The Brotherhood in Saffron: The Rashtriya Swayamsevak Sangh*

and Hindu Revivalism (New Delhi, Vistaar Publications, 1987), traces the history of the RSS and its affiliates up to 1982 with a wealth of detail, and from a position sympathetic to the Saffron brigade. Christophe Jaffrelot, *The Hindu Nationalist Movement in India* (Delhi, Penguin India, 1996; French original 1993), is more recent and carefully researched.

7 Jayaprakash Narayan (JP) had personally and publicly denied that the RSS was fascist and had praised it, instead, for its democratic struggles and, pointedly, for its role in the struggle against corruption and in favour of the poor against the rich. Upon his arrest, JP invited Nana Deshmakh, a well-known pracharak and key leader of the RSS, to take charge of his movement. This leadership role was later taken over, in November 1976, by D.B. Thengadi, a former pracharak who was then serving as the general secretary of the parivar's labour front, the Bharatiya Mazdoor Sangh.

8 The desperation of these ex-Congressmen was well grounded. In the elections of March 1977 which brought the Janata Party to power with 298 seats out of the 542 in Lok Sabha, the Jana Sangh commanded the largest component, with 93 seats, so that three RSS members – Vajpayee, Advani, and Brij Lal Vohra – became central ministers. After the assembly elections of June the same year, RSS members presided over governments in the three states of Himachal, Rajasthan, and Madhya Pradesh, and in the union territory of Delhi. It was on the coat-tails of illustrious ex-Congressmen, such as Jayaprakash and Morarji Desai, that the RSS first arrived in the halls of power.

9 The state, the bourgeoisie, the dominant media have been far more preoccupied over the past three years with the single incident of the Bombay blasts precisely because the criminal gang that is said to have engineered those blasts are Muslim; by the end of 1995, the Central Bureau of Investigations (CBI) had produced 170 chargesheets related to that lone incident, while the media have kept the memory of those blasts open like a wound. No such alacrity or alarm has been shown regarding either the destruction of the Babri mosque or the rivers of blood that have flowed in all parts of India since the rath yatra of 1991, instigated and carried out by the Hindutva forces, even though far more

substantial evidence is available about the culprits in those cases.

10 What is offered here is a generalization pertaining to a global trend. Such a broad, macro-historical generalization does not seek to explain developments in each region and country. Patterns of economic growth and political form in the East Asian region or in the oil-producing countries, for example, are obvious exceptions to these general trends.

11 In some other countries, such as Indonesia or Ghana, that kind of state had been dismantled through coups d'etat. Latin America witnessed similar reversals, culminating in the coup against Allende's socialist government in Chile, which had a decisive impact globally.

12 The literature on the rise of Islamicist radicalism since the late 1960s is vast. For the points raised here, the following may be useful: Samir Amin, 'Culture and Ideology in the Contemporary Arab World', *Rethinking Marxism*, fall 1993; Fanny Colonna, 'Cultural Resistance and Religious Legitimacy in Colonial Algeria', *Economy and Society*, 3: 3 (1974); John Howe, 'The Crisis of Algerian Nationalism and the Rise of Islamic Integralism', *New Left Review*, November-December 1992; and Saad Eddin Ibrahim, 'Anatomy of Egypt's Militant Islamic Groups', *International Journal of Middle Eastern Studies*, 12 (December 1980).

13 Andersen and Damle, The Brotherhood in Saffron, p. 50.

14 Ibid., p. 215. According to the same authors, the RSS was claiming a shakha in every one of about 5,000 villages of Kerala by 1981, which has not yet made BJP a major political force in the state but has transformed the communal situation in Kerala dramatically even though the claim itself seems to have been somewhat extravagant.

15 The next two paragraphs summarize an argument that has been presented at much greater length in 'Structure and Ideology in Italian Fascism', in *Lineages of the Present* (Delhi, Tulika, 1996).

16 The revolution in Iran has spawned a veritable industry for analyses of it. The following may be consulted more fruitfully: Ervand Abrahamian, *Iran: Between Two Revolutions* (Princeton, Princeton University Press, 1982), and *Khomeinism* (Lon-

don, I.E. Tauris, 1993); Shahrough Akhavi, *Religion and Politics in Contemporary Iran* (Albany, State University of New York, 1980); Hamid Algar (ed.), *Islam and Revolution: Writings and Statements of Imam Khomemi* (Berkley, Mizan Press, 1981); Michael Fischer, *Iran from Religious Dispute to Revolution* (Cambridge, Mass., Harvard University Press, 1980), and 'Islam and the Revolt of the Petit Bourgeoisie', *Daedalus*, Winter 1982; Azar Tabari, 'Role of Shi'i Clergy in Modern Iranian Polities', in *Khamsin* 9 (n. d.); Sami Zubaida, *Islam, the People, and the State* (London, Routledge, 1989). Nikkie R. Keddie has also authored and edited work of exceptional acumen. For a succinct comment on the disorientations of Islamic revivalisms, see Aziz Al-Azmeh, *Islams and Modernities* (London, Verso, 1993).

17 This broad agreement is signified by routine invocation of the rightwing indigenist positions of such social scientists as T.N. Madan, Ashis Nandy, and Veena Das by such subalternists as Gyanendra Pandey, Partha Chatterjee, and Dipesh Chakrabarty. Virulent attacks on secular politics are part of the shared perspective of these overlapping tendencies as they constantly seek to stage the premodern as the postmodern solution to the problems of modernity. See, for example, T.N. Madan, 'Secularism in its Place', *Journal of Asian Studies*, 46 (1987), 4; Ashis Nandy, 'An Anti-Secularist Manifesto', *Seminar* (1985), 314; Partha Chatterjee, 'Secularism and Toleration', *Economic and Political Weekly*, 29 (9 July 1994), 28; and Gyanendra Pandey, *The Construction of Communalism in Colonial North India* (New Delhi, Oxford University Press, 1990), chapter 1.

18 That anti-modernist indigenism relies heavily on the most mundane of Euro-American thought is so obvious as hardly to need documentation. For illustration, though, we may cite an essay of Ashis Nandy which is a special favourite of the subalternists: 'The Politics of Secularism and the Recovery of Religious Tolerance', in Veena Das (ed.), *Mirrors of Violence: Communities, Riots and Survivors in South Asia* (New Delhi, Oxford University Press, 1992), pp. 69-93. By the time we get to section three of the essay, 'The heart of darkness', Nandy begins with a full-blown chart in the manner of modern statisticians and behavioural psychologists, and offers an explanation of contemporary communal

violence without any reference to the actual political projects of Hindutva, without any reference to the actual events of that violence, but purely in terms of the cliches of the wholly secular, wholly Western, and modern ego psychology, overlaid, for good effect, with reference to Bogardus, Erich Fromm, Adorno, Bettelheim, someone called Milton Rokeach, and, most approvingly, Hannah Arendt and Herbert Marcuse – all of this in less than five pages.

19 See, for instance, Margaret C. Jacob, *The Radical Enlightenment: Pantheists, Freemasons and Republicans* (London, George Alien and Unwin, 1981), which also includes a most useful bibliographical essay on the subject. In his work on the eighteenth century, and later in his book on Blake – *Witness against the Beast: William Blake and the Moral Law* (Cambridge, Cambridge University Press, 1993) – E. P. Thompson points out time and again the extreme complexity of an 'Enlightenment' that came to be identified only retrospectively, by the middle of the nineteenth century, with 'rationalism'.

20 Needless to add that Locke's social contract did not envisage rights of representation for women and the propertyless, and that Mill's radical individualism, verging on libertarianism, excluded the colonized. 'Despotism', he says, 'is a legitimate [form] of government when dealing with barbarians' – meaning of course, the non-European and the colonized.

21 Mary Wollstonecraft and others were to soon enquire: what, then, is the gender of 'Citizen'? Thus began that productive dialogue between feminism and the Enlightenment that is yet to be concluded.

22 For a brilliant and closely argued text on this theme, though with emphases rather different from the ones I have briefly picked up on here, see Etienne Balibar, 'Citizen Subject', in Eduardo Cadava et al. (eds), *Who Comes after the Subject?* (New York, Routledge, 1991). See also chapters 2 and 9 in Etienne Balibar, *Masses, Classes, Ideas: Studies on Politics and Philosophy before and after Marx* (London, Routledge, 1993).

23 As he puts it in Emile: 'He who wishes to keep the first place in the civil order for the feelings of nature does not know what

he wants... he can never be either man or citizen. He can be no good to himself, or to others.'

24 In Rousseau's own words, 'you are undone if you once forget that the fruits of the earth belong to us all, and the earth itself to nobody'.

25 Colletti argues convincingly that despite all the emphasis on the priority of the social over the individual, Rousseau's thought finally remains within the confines of individualism. See the closing pages of his careful treatment of this subject in Lucio Colletti, *From Rousseau to Lenin* (New York, Monthly Review Press, 1972).

Right-Wing Politics, and the Cultures of Cruelty

I want to thank you for giving me this opportunity to deliver the Ved Gupta Memorial Lecture this year.[1] Unfortunately, I never had the privilege of knowing the late Mr. Gupta. I am nevertheless gratified to be speaking in the memory of a man who gave so much of his energy and passion to the building of a culture of broad democratic values, at a time when values of a democratic culture are under greater assault and stress than ever before. Later in this lecture, I shall be arguing that the current assault on our educational and research institutions is designed specifically to permeate the educated sections of society with politics of hate and cultures of cruelty in the service of a rightwing project for which the word 'fascist' seems appropriate.[2] I shall be using this word repeatedly throughout this lecture. So, let me start by reflecting on the meaning and salience of this word.

There are three perfectly correct but quite distinct ways of using this word. One is the colloquial one, in which we sometimes use the word 'fascist', when we are righteously angry and when we mean to be abusive, for any particularly repugnant act of cruelty, violence or repression, certainly in public life but also in what are generally understood as personal relations. At the opposite end is the most strictly accurate usage of the term, whereby, really, only the Mussolini regime in Italy could be called fascist; Nazis were not, Franco's dictatorship in Spain was not, and the Sangh parivar evidently is not. But then there is also a third usage, by no means uncommon or inappropriate, but more supple and wide-ranging, in which the word 'fascism' is used to negotiate a very complex experience, spanning a whole century and virtually the whole world, in which a wide range of ideologies, movements and regimes have arisen which are not exactly the same, so that it becomes irrelevant to speak of a singular 'fascist paradigm' to which all of them correspond, but which are in some fundamental way of the same design and frequently of the same inspiration.

It is in this last sense that the origins of fascism are traceable not merely to Italy after the First World War but also to France in the last quarter of the 19th century,[3] and that we speak of the resurgence of fascism across the whole of Western Europe today,[4] or of the rise to power of the descendants of fascism in the four main states that have arisen from the ruins of former Yugoslavia.[5] Also, it is in this sense that I have used the term clerical-fascist for the Islamic regime in Iran since Khomeini's seizure of power some two decades ago, or that the Hindutva brand of nationalism appears to me to be intrinsically fascist in character. The word 'fascism' in this usage is not an exercise in paradigm-building or a particularly strong mode of denunciation. Rather, it designates certain forms of politics that have been with us, on the global scale, since roughly the 1880s, which is also the moment of the birth of modern imperialism on the one hand, and the moment of the emergence of mass working class parties on the other. The word itself of course came much later, but that this kind of politics and ideology should arise alongside modern imperialism and the modern revolutionary movements is by no means a coincidence, just as it is no coincidence that the RSS was formed roughly at the same time when the anti-colonial movement first became a mass movement and certain kinds of working class politics of the Left got going.[6] The sum of ideologies for which the word 'fascist' seems appropriate are ideologies that belong specifically to the age of imperialism, anti-imperialism and revolutionary class struggle, and, as I shall argue later, fundamental to these forms of politics has been the will to fashion an anti-materialist conception of revolution, anti-liberal conception of nationalism, anti-rationalist critique of Modernity, anti-humanist assaults on the politics of liberation, in a rhetoric of "blood and belonging", and in the name of a glorious past that never was. These are ideologies of a revolutionary age, pre-emptive and counter-revolutionary ideologies of course, but these too are dedicated to making their own kind of revolutions – that is, revolutions of the Far Right. The fundamental premise of my argument today is that India is at present undergoing a revolutionary process. We do not recognise it as such because it is a revolution not of the Left but of the Far Right – of the sort that is currently under way in Algeria, for example. Whether this revolution shall fail or succeed is far from clear, nor is it at all clear that even the simple territorial unity of the country shall survive the fires that this offensive has lit. The cultures of cruelty that are spreading all around us are a part of this Far Right revolutionary offensive because values of democratic, secular civility must be made to crumble from the inside; and that is so because, in the conditions of electoral and parliamentary democracy prevailing in India today, what the Far Right visualizes and prepares for is not a frontal seizure of power but a hurricane from below, carried out by a widespread and pliable mass of the wretched of this earth led by a well-disciplined counter-revolutionary elite.

I have written elsewhere, more or less polemically, that every country gets the fascism that it deserves, by which I simply mean that the specific form that a fascist movement takes shall always depend on the social physiognomy of that country: that is to say, the economic, political, philosophical, aesthetic, religious, cultural and ideological forms that are specific to that country.[7] India is no exception to this rule, and to identify the forms specific to our experience we have to look downward and inward. But the Indian experience cannot be extricated from the experience of the modern world as a whole – the world that begins, politically speaking, in one sense with the French Revolution during the last quarter of the 18th century, and in another sense with the onset of modern imperialism a century later during the last quarter of the 19th century, and in another sense with the collapse of communism in the closing decades of the present century. Our own experiences of colonisation, independence and what we now call 'liberalisation' are a part of this larger story. It is in order to locate the phenomenon of fascism in this larger story that I have reminded you of the actual origins of this kind of politics in late nineteenth century. I should also want to offer a certain principle of periodisation for our experience of fascism during the present century, which is based on a contrast that runs as follows. Fascism of course remains a punctual but subordinate political tendency throughout the whole of the imperialist period. However, there have been two quite different historical moments when the epidemic of such movements has become particularly widespread, for somewhat different structural reasons. Thus, we might say that the fascisms of the inter-war period corresponded to the crises of accumulation brought about by the maturing of imperialism itself as it made a fuller transition from the competitive to the monopoly structure of capital. This is an explanation that Baran and Sweezy, among others, and Poulantzas in his own way, have accepted; and I would add that whereas movements of this kind were particularly strong in the core countries of Europe, their influence spread through much of the world, from Japan to Iraq, Syria and Lebanon, and from Argentina to India. By contrast, the end-of-the-century fascisms of today correspond to the Late Imperial period of full globalization of the capitalist mode, in which the mode has provisionally triumphed over communist states but faces internal crises of stagnation in the core countries and unmanageable social tensions in the less industrialised countries, brought about in part by that imperialist globalization and in part by the defeat or decay of the socialist, democratic and secular-nationalist projects within the imperialized countries.

I draw your attention to this principle of periodisation for three reasons. First, to emphasize that since the fascisms of today belong in an entirely novel period of modern history they cannot repeat the experience and the forms of an earlier and very different period. They have to be understood both in terms of their lineage as well as their particularity. Second, the characterisation of the later, more contemporary phase helps us understand a certain reversal, namely that whereas the scale of violence in such malignant movements has been relatively more manageable for the constitutional governments of Western Europe, they have erupted with far greater ferocity in the peripheries of the system where conditions of crisis are more advanced: especially in some central European and Asian zones including, notably, India. Whether or not Russia will go the way of Serbia is yet not clear. Third, this sense of the scope of malignancy also clarifies that what we are dealing with here is not some kind of Indian exceptionalism but a generalized experience of our time that is taking specific forms in our own country.

That is the first point: fascism as a *generalized* tendency throughout the history of imperialism, but a tendency that takes different forms in different national conditions, while the history of imperialism itself needs to be understood in terms of distinct phases and periods within this larger history. But, then, all fascisms have at their core a pathological form of nationalism. Indeed, this type of ideology was called 'integral nationalism' in France before it came to be called 'fascism' in Italy. This pathology is as much there in the Hindutva brand of nationalism as in the National Front in France or the National Alliance in Italy or the sundry projects of national purification and ethnic cleansing that have been going on in various parts of the former Yugoslavia, not to speak of the classical variety in Italy and Germany, from which some of the founders of Hindutva, such as Savarkar and Moonje, drew so much inspiration. Now, the fact that fascism itself rests on a pathological variety of nationalism requires that we reflect on the phenomenon of nationalism itself. Yet, in the intellectual climate prevailing today, it is very difficult to discuss the subject of nationalism. There once was a time, in the period of anti-colonial struggles, when all varieties of nationalism were presumed to be good. Then, as a certain disillusionment with the nationalism of the national bourgeoisie began to set in,[8] and as anti-rationalist critiques of Modernity began to be assembled in the metropolitan countries,[9] it transpired that anti-colonialism was nothing more than the other face of colonialism itself – a colonial discourse, to be exact.[10] In the Indian context, it is significant that a quasi-radical indictment of the Nehruvian model of economic nationalism was forged at exactly the same time when the Right wing indictment of Nehruvian secularism was beginning to make inroads among the *haute intelligentsia*; later, of course, the two indictments, of planned development and of secularism, were to converge.[11] Meanwhile, the high ground of nationalist claim, which had earlier been associated mainly with national liberation struggles and anti-colonial movements, came to be occupied increasingly by radicalisms of the Right, more murderous in some places than others, not just in East and Central Europe after the collapse of communism there but also in great many places across Asia and Africa, notably Iran, Afghanistan and India. It was in this larger context that nationalism – all of it, all varieties of it – fell into terrible disrepute.

This has been very bewildering for someone such as myself who has been deeply suspicious of the pathologies of fascistic nationalism but who also believes in at least two other things. The first is that in a backward capitalist country like India, which is socially more heterogeneous than any other country on earth, and which is undergoing enormous stresses as it undertakes very haphazard, very hit-and-miss kind of modernisation of its anachronistic structures, nationalism is simply a necessary cement if the country is not to fall apart; if the Left fails to harness this energy and provide that cement, the Right most assuredly shall. But, then, I also believe that in an age of imperialism, a Leftist kind of nationalism is an objective necessity. To the extent that it is the nation-state that facilitates the imperialist penetrations of the economy and guarantees the various prevailing regimes of labour, the nation-state remains the necessary horizon of politics, and it is important that we not concede the ground of nationalism to the rightwing.

How does one then come to terms with this whole range within nationalism, from the revolutionary to the pathological, from the democratic to the fascist. I was saying a bit earlier that if mass politics of the working class, fascism and modern imperialism are the issue, then perhaps the 1880s, roughly, can be regarded as the point of departure. But if we were to trace the genealogies of nations and nationalisms, the point of departure shall have to be moved to a point a century or so earlier, in and around the French Revolution. It was then that all manner of nationalisms that are still with us were born. Not all of them are the gift of the Enlightenment; many are mere pathologies of the Romantic imagination – but it is then, in that great revolutionary upheaval at the origin of the modern world, that the fundamental bifurcation takes place.

Here I shall offer you not a periodisation but a typology, necessarily schematic, not about the history of nationalism but about its ideological formation. At the most general level, and contrary to what one has learned in certain kinds of Marxism, it needs to be said that nationalism *per se* is not a class ideology and that the political character of any given nationalism depends on the nature of the power bloc that takes hold of it and utilises it for its own dominance. As such, there are progressive nationalisms and retrogressive nationalisms; more frequently, any given nationalism tends to be progressive and retrogressive at the same time, with regard to one social reality or the other. An anti-colonial nationalism is perfectly capable, for example, of accommodating a high degree of xenophobia or settled prejudices against women. Among the many processes that have gone into the making of this complex history, I should want to isolate two conceptual moments that are analytically separable but appear in real history in varying combinations.

On the one hand, the modern *constitutional* state that rests upon the idea of the nation arose initially as a profane civil entity, against religious authority and monarchical or feudal or even colonial autocracy. In the conception of the nation that derives from the French 'Declaration of Rights of Man and the Citizen' the idea of citizenship is radically separated from race, religion or any other kind of primordial belonging, and is made much looser, available to all who are willing to accept the authority of the nation-state and the rights and obligations that apply to all equally and universally. The emergence of this conception of the nation marks the transition from subjection to citizenship, from obligation to rights, and constitutes a realm of political action and legislative function based on some modern conception of legitimacy, associated usually with popular representation. This realm of citizenship is then seen as an active ingredient in agencies for social change, be it revolutionary or reformist. From Hegel to Croce to Gramsci, there is a strong tradition of requiring from the nation-state that it should punctually act as an ethical, pedagogical function designed to serve people's needs for reform and progress in the various social and economic domains. One may designate this as the Enlightenment conception of the state, in the original sense of a rationalist project that was often expressed in Idealist terms. Even the Leninist conception which squarely identifies the revolutionary moment as the moment of the smashing of the state rests on the notion of the need to create an alternate form of state, the proletarian state, as the ethical form for the transition toward a classless society. In none of these conceptions is the nation-state regarded as the expression of an *ethnos*, a condition of the soul, an expression of *culture*, a matter of religious identity and primordial belonging. A nation is emphatically not a race. From Rousseau and Kant to Lenin, this type of state has been associated with rational plans for creating the good society, while citizenship in a nation is seen as transitional toward an eventually universal society. In Marx, of course, there is a deep distrust of the division of humanity into nations and states, even though, as the *Manifesto* emphasized, every proletariat has to settle accounts, first of all, with its own bourgeoisie.

The other contrasting moment in the making of modern nations and nationalisms is descended essentially from that tendency in German Idealism that is most forcefully represented by Herder and Fichte. Upon re-reading it recently, I was quite struck by the fact that in *A History of Western Philosophy*, a book written as far ago as 1945, Bertrand Russell associates Fichte with right-wing romanticism on the one hand, and with Nietzsche on the other, and characterises him as a prophet of what Russell calls "nationalistic totalitarianism". In this alternative conception, the state embodies a general will arising not out of a common citizenship but out of a cultural essence, based on ethnicity, race, religion, language or some other form of a primordial intimacy specific to an entity that by definition excludes others. In this conception, there is a sharp distinction between the national Self and the rest of the world; citizenship in such a nation is conceived not in terms of expanding toward a universalist inclusion but in terms of self-definition, enclosure, even self-purification. This conceptual universe rests, ultimately, on cultural wars and civilizing missions; and on the obliteration of heterogeneity to obtain homogeneous nations. More often than not, such conceptions of the nation have been prone to xenophobia, irrationalism, cultural differentialism, racism, and relativisms of all sorts.

Between these competing notions of the nation-state I undoubtedly prefer the universalist and inclusivist conception which rests on the criterion not of primordial difference but of modern citizenship. Having offered you so sharp a distinction, however, let me immediately add that this is a typology, constructed for methodological purposes, not for a strict or accurate description of the real. These are essentially poles of attraction, and rare is a nationalism that gravitates only to one pole or the other. What one needs to grasp, when one is trying to grasp the real, is the exact combination and the range, because the range within the practices of most nationalisms tends to be usually very wide. Our historical experience is that most anti-colonial nationalisms tend to be ideological hybrids. On the one hand, these are forward-looking movements specifically of the modern kind, in the sense that their entire ideological articulation is based on a very modern conception of every people's inherent right to liberty, collective self-determination and popular sovereignty. This aspect of anti-colonial movements aligns them with the rationalist and democratic aspects of the Enlightenment project and the libertarian legacy of the French Revolution. However, every nationalism of the defeated also has an inherent potential for revivalist nostalgia and national re-purification, since foreign rule is experienced ideologically as a violation of the collective identity, imposition of alien cultural forms, and a fall from a past greatness. And, to the extent that the privileged intelligentsia, especially in a caste-ridden society such as India, tends to confuse culture with religion, the slide from dreams of cultural retrieval to religious revivalism, and from cultural nationalism to religious purification and particularity, always lurks as a real potential at the very heart of anti-colonial nationalisms of the bourgeois and petty bourgeois strata. The rationalist and the Romantic elements of the imagination, the traditionalising and the modernizing impulses in projects of social change, exist *simultaneously* in any nationalism of the defeated, and one needs to examine any particular nationalism carefully so as to determine as to which side within this contradictory unity is dominant.

This makes very problematic the kind of opposition we normally proclaim between the communal and the secular in India. I am not referring here simply to those quite numerous individuals, especially among the professional politicians but also more generally among the urban sophisticates of the privileged classes, who are secularists one day and communalist the next. They are in reality neither the one nor the other. They are rank opportunists, and they often are, in the word that Mussolini was fond of using for himself, "super-relativists". I mean something much more complex. On the one hand, the entire history of what we call our secular nationalism is replete with nostalgic revivalisms and those claims of cultural particularity which trace themselves back to a Golden Age when India was pristinely Hindu, undisturbed by Christian and Muslim intrusions; it is possible to call this nationalism secular, though with much reservation and difficulty, only because that same formation also had, as a dominant element within itself, a vision of a modern, post-colonial India that was culturally diverse, religiously pluralistic, constitutionally federalist and republican, with extensive guarantees of individual and collective rights. The formative years of the Republic were undoubtedly marked by a nationalism which was essentially universalist and inclusive, hence largely capable of controlling its own impulses toward revivalism. On the other hand, however, revivalist tendencies were very powerful in their own right, as organized political forces such as the Hindu Mahasabha and the RSS, as subordinate ideological formations within the mainly secular nationalism, and as elements in diverse reform movements, educational societies, literary and linguistic projects, and so on. In short, then, the terrain of nationalism in

India has always been a contested terrain, over which the secular and the communal have struggled as opposing forces but also as adjacent plants growing on the same soil. Just as much secular nationalism tended to be nostalgic and revivalist in the cultural domain without becoming politically communal, much of communal politics saw itself as a redemptive project in pursuit of a primordial essence that was perceived as the true cement for the national compact. For the communalist, therefore, it was perfectly possible to see himself as a true nationalist in so far as he could perceive himself as a crusader on behalf of the overwhelming numerical majority in the nation. This nationalistic subjectivity of a communalist I should want to illustrate briefly, before returning to a more methodical statement a bit later.

Let me suggest to you, more or less provocatively, that when Mr. Advani, at present our Home Minister, claims that he is a secular man, he is by his own lights perhaps right; he is not notably devout, except nominally for purposes of Hindutva mobilizations; there is little reason to believe that he wishes to impose here in India a theocracy of the type that the Irani mullahs, or worse still the Afghani Taliban, desire for their respective countries; and I would tend to think – I don't know for sure, but it is probably the case – that he is perfectly secular in relation to other Hindus and perhaps even some non-Hindus of his choice. The problem of his communalism is pre-eminently a problem of his relationship with the *generality* of non-Hindus. Some sources of this problem we can mention, for illustrative purposes. One is a confusion of categories: he mistakes religion for culture and culture for nation, hence the further confusion between private belief and rights of citizenship. Second, he seems to have a wrong kind of belief in arithmetic. He mistakes citizenship for a numerical calculation; more must have more rights, fewer can live with fewer rights. He seems not to understand that in a civilized society the reverse often has to be the case; a social majority can make do with general and equal rights alone, whereas it is the social minority that lives with very real possibilities and fears of infringement and therefore needs some extra safeguards. And, he believes too much in blood – and in *varieties* of blood. The spilling of the blood of non-Hindus leaves him quite evidently unper-turbed; the spilling of the blood of a Hindu fills him with a very special kind of passion and with great agitations of the soul. He is obviously very skillful at perpetrating culture wars and he equally obviously thinks of the RSS as a civilizing mission. Conversions disturb him because he evidently thinks of religion as a kind of race and religious conversion as a kind of racial miscegenation, contrary to the purity and primordiality of belief and belonging. The poorest adivasi, whom the Hindu caste society has never taken into its own fold, is still a part of this primordiality and becomes a nominal Hindu, retrospectively, as soon as he converts to a religion that entered India, in the remote past, from elsewhere. Like his other colleagues in the RSS, Mr. Advani seems to believe that the territorial boundary is also the boundary, the permanent boundary, between the sacred and the profane. This odd identification between territory, blood and belief is what requires that this defilement by religious conversion be stopped and undone. The ones who have undertaken these sacraments of purification, through rituals of fire and murder, are the heroes of the nation. Thus it is that he can calmly certify the goons of the Bajrang Dal as true nationalists. I am sure that those goons also regard Mr. Advani as a great nationalist. The admiration, the certification, is undoubtedly mutual.

Now, for a secularist such as myself, that kind of judgement is much easier to make. What is infinitely more difficult to assess is the meandering, contradictory history of what we call our secular nationalism. I shall come to the specifics soon, but let me first offer you the proposition that secularism is a revolutionary ideal and a modern civic virtue. It does not arise spontaneously out of a traditional society. Most traditional societies, certainly the settled agrarianate societies, are deeply hierarchical, tolerant and intolerant at the same time: tolerant of some differences and intolerant of some others, usually with wide fluctuations, even though clear and stable lines of demarcation and hierarchy are attempted all the time. Demarcations between castes, classes and genders, in the absence of any common conception of juridic equalities, give to such societies a deeply intolerant character. At their most tolerant, however, traditional societies practise a kind of benign pluralism among communities and a kind of benign neglect of a whole range of religious differences among individuals. This kind of toleration is surely a mode of social decency, much to be valued but not to be confused with what one could reasonably call secularism. The fact is worth contemplating that within Europe itself, from where most of our ideas of constitutional governance have come, secularism got enshrined as a constitutional obligation in procedures of governance only in the wake of a massive revolutionary upheaval in France; and the translation of the formal juridic equality of denominationally different persons into a substantive social equality is still very far from having become a finished achievement. Ask any Jew, and you will find out that living in Europe has been for her a living hell in the modern as much as in the premodern periods, right up to the end of the Second World War. Civic equality for European or American Jews is a phenomenon of only the last half a century, an experience that the generality of blacks are yet to take for granted in the United States, so that when a Muslim friend once asked me in what respect the experience of Muslims in India was really different than that of American blacks, I was left rather speechless. What I am trying to say is that the struggle to obtain a society based on civic, secular equalities – let alone a society of equality in the domain of economic entitlements – requires revolutionary transformations and has so far been very difficult to obtain.

Now, it is very much a virtue of our constitutional covenant that it is based on conceptions of radical juridic equalities, which encompasses a whole range of social equalities including secular equalities. This Constitution is one of the finest documents in the long history of that global revolution that first began in France two hundred years ago and which too is yet very far from finished. I don't want to at all minimize the great value of this collective possession of ours. But I would submit to you that if we really want to understand the actual character of the Indian state we should equally examine the actual practices of the Police, the Provincial Constabularies, the other agencies of state as they operate on the ground. That is where the limits of our democracy and our secularism are the most palpable. These routinised violences of the state agencies, including their routinised participation in communal violence, their methodical neglect to investigate or punish communal violence, are not merely epiphenomenal. So substantial a part of the daily conduct of agencies of the state can never be epiphenomenal. One cannot take comfort in supposing that all this is a consequence of the degeneration of the political elite and the professional politicians. In part, it is a consequence of such degenerations. But no state, certainly no state based on electoral democracy, is ever so very epiphenomenal, so very much outside and above civil society, that its widespread personnel, which has to live within that very civil society, can go on participating in certain kinds of violences which have no substantial sanction within that society.

When the police oppresses the poor peasants and the landless peasantry, we know that the whole power and system of property – property in general – stands behind that police. When we think of the routinised violences that are perpetrated against women in society, we know that it is not a matter, in the final analysis, of this or that individual but of the patriarchal structure as a whole. We know, or at least most of us contrive to know, the same about caste violences. And we know that agencies of state are fully implicated in these other kinds of violences precisely because they have a wide social sanction. Might it not be the case that communal violence also has a much wider social sanction behind it than we have heretofore acknowledged? That is the question that undercuts the common, comforting belief that most of our society is really tolerant and secular, or that communal violence is simply a sectional and marginal pathology. So, when I use the phrase "cultures of cruelty" I mean something more than professional politicians, more than agencies of the state on the ground, more even than organized communalism; I mean a much wider web of social sanctions in which one kind of violence can be tolerated all the more because many other kinds of violence are tolerated anyway. Dowry deaths do facilitate the burning of women out of communal motivations, and, together, these two kinds of violences do contribute to the making of a more generalised culture of cruelty as well as a more generalized ethical numbness toward cruelty as such. And when I speak of "right-wing politics and the cultures of cruelty", I undoubtedly refer to the culture of cruelties that the Hindutva right-wing is creating, methodically and in cold blood, in pursuit of what strikes me as a fascist project. I do mean that such cultures of cruelty have been a punctual feature of the politics of the far right throughout its history, everywhere in the world. I do mean to draw your attention to the great discrepancy between the spiritualist claim of defending Hindu piety, Hindu tradition, Hindu ethos, and the creation in practice of a brutish and brutalising culture as is symbolised by the average member of the Bajrang Dal, who functions as a storm trooper of the Hindutva purification over which our Prime Minister, the liberal Mr. Vajpayee, is pleased to preside. But I also mean something else, that the hindutva brigade is not only an agent and a perpetrator, it is also a beneficiary. If it acts *upon* the wider culture so as to brutalize it, the pre-existing cultures of cruelty also serve to sustain its projects.

That much, I thought, I should say. But what about our 'secular nationalism'? This is my own tradition; it has had a powerful presence and on the whole a positive role in our society; it is what prevented India, in the midst of the communal holocaust that accompanied the Partition, from becoming a Hindu Rashtra and gave to the country a democratic, secular constitution. You would be misunderstanding me completely if you were to conclude that I wish to downplay or disregard this tradition. It is mine; it has made me what I am. It is yours, and it has made you what you are. Mr. Ved Gupta is no longer among us, but if I understand the meaning of his life correctly he too would have been proud to belong to it. And yet, because this tradition is ours – this tradition that tries so very hard to live up to the ethical claims of a modern rationality – we have the birthright to criticize it, as severely as we wish, in the spirit of that Enlightenment which has taught us that the exercise of one's own critical faculty is not only a right but a duty, without the performance of which the good society cannot come into being. So, let me also say the following, in the spirit of a self-criticism, more or less.

When I emphasized that secularism does not arise spontaneously out of the traditional society but is a modern civic virtue that had come into being as part of a project to revolutionize society as a whole, I wanted to draw your attention to quite a few things. One is that modern politics in India began not as an exercise in citizenship, since no one can be the citizen of a colony, but as so many attempts to organize pressure groups that could negotiate with the colonial authority, and, inevitably, these pressure groups were organized around the fault lines that existed already in society, so that factors of religion, caste and community were paramount in the organisation of such groups. For all its attempts and claims to become secular, even the Indian National Congress, when it arose, was itself constantly attempting to reach some sort of a balance among elites of various religious entities and denominational communities. I would even suggest to you that diverse individuals and groups subscribing to a particular religion or sect came to be defined as coherent communities and political entities precisely because groups of elites needed to claim that they represented such communities and entities. In the colonial society, community was where citizenship was not. The very idea that we now take as self-evident, that Hindus and Muslims and Christians respectively constitute homogeneous and politically meaningful communities, is the product of that fantastic moment when the representors had to invent the represented. In that semi-modernizing society of non-citizenship, nationalism in its originary moment could only be cultural nationalism because it was politically too weak to claim an identity as a politically formed nation. Please contemplate the fact that the claim that we are a nation is, in our history, much older than the claim that we are a *secular* nation or that this nationhood in some fundamental way cannot be born without the abolition of colonial autocracy. Even the most secular of our nationalists continued to think of India as a primordial nation civilizationally defined, rather than a modern nation that was the *product* of the anti-colonial movement itself and an entity that arose out of the crucible of 15 August 1947. In such conceptions, the nation was already an embodiment of a supposed shared culture and not a product of common citizenship or juridic equality. Our nationalism was cultural well before it was political or civic or secular. In this ambience, the temptations of blood and belonging, of spiritual essence, of racial or religious particularity, of revivalism and purification were particularly strong. Religious identity was built into our canonical reform movements and into even the prehistory of Indian nationalism, as these evolved not only in Bengal but also elsewhere, as for example among the Muslim reformists of North India, not to speak of the Muslim political elite as a whole, throughout the history of that anti-colonial and communally marked nationalism; as much those who participated in the separatist movement as the ones who were absorbed in Congress nationalism; Jinnah and Azad, after all, equally insisted on being Muslims and leaders of Muslims, the only complication being that they offered different recipes for the Muslims whom both claimed to represent.

All of this was very much complicated by the caste and class character of these reformers, revivalists and cultural nationalists. This caste and class origin necessarily *required* a misrecognition of the actual character of the people who were now said to be a nation. The Orientalist scholarship which gave us the images of Aryan origin, Vedic purity and Muslim tyranny was in fact a joint product of some bookish Europeans and these upper caste gentlemen, with equal though different investment in such images. So, the nostalgia that arose out of such scholarship had a peculiarly strong caste flavour; the India of the past was the past of these upper castes. The revivalisms were not even *national* in any substantive fashion; as Gramsci immortally remarked, the word "nation" means nothing if it does not mean "the people". For those gentlemen-reformers, however, 'the people' remained a rhetorical category, always to be invoked but never granted any autonomous space in those projects of reform, while the reforms that were proposed or undertaken in the name of the nation always remained confined to their own class, caste and/or community. So, the line between reform and revivalism remained forever blurred, and the revivalisms as such were just so many narcissisms of those upper castes that could no longer rule in reality and therefore ruled only in the imagination, not in the present but in a past that was somehow to be transformed into a future. The only thing that guaranteed the security of this phantasy was the fact of property, which they still commanded, as they had commanded in the past; here, then, was the real link between their past and their present, which they hoped to continue into the future. Colonial government was acceptable because it was now the real guarantor of that property. Those early heroes of ours were conservative, socially and politically, and not even notably anti-colonial. In this milieu, then, our nationalism was born.

I shall take up this story again in a moment. What I have just said prompts me to offer you two observations, however. One is the reminder of what Hegel once said, namely that only the slave can understand the whole of society because he must understand himself as well as the conditions of his exploitation, and hence his master; whereas the master can rest his laurels on understanding merely himself and the terms on which he can exploit his slave. It is in this specific sense that the consciousness of the subjugated is always superior to the consciousness of the rulers. Which leads me to my second observation, namely that in the multiplicity of our reform movements, it was only the reform movements of the oppressed castes, and the efforts of some valiant women, that were substantially free of those kinds of revivalisms and had some fundamental understanding of the social whole, and therefore of the "nation" conceived as "the people", because the overwhelming majority of "the people" were neither upper class nor upper caste. It is no wonder that among all the reformists Periyar stands out as an avowed atheist and Ambedkar ultimately undertook a formal religious conversion not as merely a personal act but as a public and participatory act, living his conversion not as a personal salvation but as militant repudiation of caste society and as an invitation to mass repudiation of the same. At this dangerous turn in our history when Mr. Vajpayee recommends a national debate on the issue of conversions, I would suggest to you that, in the larger historical sense, there is something that connects the spirit of our Constitution, which calls upon us to abolish caste and denomination as politically meaningful categories, and the spirit in which Ambedkar, the principal architect of that Constitution, undertook his own departure from caste society and led a mass conversion out of that kind of slavery. In this moment, when a spiral of fire that burns crosses as well as Christians is flaming across the country, it is important for us to say that there have been in our history, in the remote past and in the recent past, religious conversions – out of caste society, and sometimes out of religion altogether – that we must take up as so many badges of revolt and honour.

But I was talking about that originary moment when revivalism and a nostalgia for a golden age in the past was rampant among impressive sections of the intelligentsia that defined the first rudiments of cultural nationalism. Precisely at the time, during the closing years of the nineteenth century and the opening ones of the twentieth, when representatives of Indian economic nationalism were formulating analytic procedures for explaining colonial exploitations, some of the most influential figures in the literary and cultural fields were deeply attracted by a cultural nationalism that was distinctly revivalist in character and religiously exclusivist by implication. Neither Bankim nor Aurobindo, neither the Swadeshi Movement in Bengal nor the Shivaji cult propagated in Maharashtra by such icons of Indian nationalism as Tilak himself, were quite untainted by that kind of revivalist fervour. Indeed, so powerful was the revivalist culture of the upper castes that when anti-Brahminical movements surfaced in Maharashtra, whether under Phule or Ambedkar, it was the extremity of the backlash of the upper castes in that region that gave us the RSS in the first place, with all its mythologies of blood and belief.

This is not to say that either Tilak or Aurobindo would be quite approving of what the Hindutva of our own day is and does. And yet there is enough there for a common sense to prevail today among sections of the urban upper castes and middle classes, in various parts of India, especially the Northern and the Western, to be persuaded that the social vision and cultural idiom of this modern-day Hindutva is descended from that general ambience of our 'renaissance' and 'awakening'.

Indeed the potentials of that kind of revivalism were so pernicious that Tagore was to warn at length, already in the second decade of this century, that there was only a short step from revivalist zealotry to communal frenzy. In two of his great novels, *Gora* and *Home and the World*, whatever other shortcomings those novels might also have, Tagore was to portray with great sensitivity and acumen how revivalist politics and communal closures may be particularly tempting to the socially insecure and the upwardly mobile.

That, then, is a crucial point: the sheer persistence of Brahminical revivalisms at the very heart of what were expected to be structures of our modernity and which never did give us any kind of modernity, precisely because of the extensive compromises they made with colonial representations of Indian history and because of their interest in representing their caste cultures as our 'national culture'. Hindutva has derived much comfort from those revivalisms, but considerable sections of what we call our secular nationalism have never been quite free of that kind of rhetoric, so much so that *Hind Swaraj* is of course a major document of that nostalgia fantasy of the past but even Nehru's *Discovery of India* tends sometimes to rehearse precisely those themes. There have of course been many valiant individuals, even some groupings, for whom secularism has been a primary value but, for the most part, what passes for secularism in India is in fact a tolerant kind of pluralism, which has tended to in fact accentuate the role of religion in public life rather than bring about its decline, and the Iftar party in which the Muslim Mullah can embrace Madan Lal Khurana is of course one of the more humorous, one of the more bizarre expressions of this professed pluralism. In this larger context, then, one can say that it is only on the Left that a whole political formation has arisen for which secularism is a fundamental premise.

So we have been caught between the rising tide of revivalist communalism on the Right, a tolerant kind of pluralism on the part of a Centre that has been collapsing and fragmenting for a couple of decades now, and a Left that has been a substantial presence but still a minority current in society as a whole, the only redeeming feature being that the Left commands a moral authority and a degree of social consent very much exceeding its numerical strength. It is in this context that the Sangh undertakes wave after wave of its offensives and dreams of completing its revolution of the Far Right within the foreseeable future. It creates a widespread culture of cruelty so that the violences it desires may be carried out not only by its actual members but also by the mobs and the vagrants whom it incites, assembles and motivates.

I said a bit earlier that a common trait among movements of this kind is that they offer an anti-materialist conception of revolution, an anti-liberal conception of nationalism, and an anti-rationalist critique of Modernity. Let me briefly explain what I mean. Historically, these movements arose in response to the emergence of mass working class parties which offered a materialist conception of revolution, based on an understanding that the real history was the history of material production and therefore of the classes that were engaged in those productions and their benefits. This conception posited the primacy of class conflict, with a vision of multi-cultural and multi-religious unities of the working class, and a revolutionary restructuring of society based on economic and social justice and the collective management of the production of wealth by an association of the direct producers. In this conception, the state was to be reduced eventually to a purely managerial function, and nations themselves amalgamated into a universalist equality. Movements of integral nationalism, and then of fascism, arose in direct opposition to each and all of these propositions. Real history, they said, is the history of culture, belief, blood, race, language and what I have called primordial intimacy. The true revolution was the one that affirmed and purified this fundamental nature and ethos of the nation, and for this purification one needed not a weakened but a vastly strengthened militarised nation. What was primary was not the domains of production or the conflict of classes but the domains of subjectivity and identity, be they racial or religious or linguistic, and the real clash was the civilizational clash of these identities. The real arena of struggle was not the material but the spiritual; and the real motivating force was not reason or even ethics but the spirit, the imagination, the myth.

And this kind of nationalism was an anti-liberal nationalism in a very specific sense. The *economic* project of liberalism, the project of private property and the market and the accumulation of capital, were accepted and posited against the collectivist economic project of the working class parties. But the *political* project of liberalism – based as it was on individual freedoms, broad tolerance of religious and cultural diversities, and representative forms of government – was rejected as inadequate for the tasks of radical re-structuring of the nation which required not individual freedom but mass consent to a homogeneous culture and the superiority of one religion over another, one race over another. It is significant that the Jews who came in for such a special treatment by the Nazis were perceived as aliens on both counts, race as well as religion. Against parliamentary democracy, these movements upheld authoritarian command structures, a cult of the leader, a cult of violence as a necessary means of purification, a virtually paramilitary organization of their cadres and an extra-parliamentary structure of the core leadership group, a culture of obedience among the cadres and of spectacular mobilizations of the masses. The March on Rome, the burning of the Reichstag, the shilanyas, the rath yatras, the spectacular destruction of Mir Baqi's antique little mosque – these are events in a single chain. And it is sobering to recall that the shakhas of the RSS in India were consciously patterned after the fascist training centres in Italy, after Moonje had visited those centres and had chatted with Mussolini.

Likewise the anti-rationalist critique of Modernity! It is significant that this critique of Modernity was also very partial. It does not include, for example, a repudiation of the market, which has been so central an institution of capitalist forms of rationality and modernity. Nor does it repudiate the sciences and technologies upon which modern industrial production is based, and which are so much the source of capitalist wealth. Rather, it rejects what Eric Hobsbawm has felicitously called 'the Enlightenment Left': the values of non-racial and non-denominational equality, the fraternity of the culturally diverse, the supremacy of Reason over Faith, the belief in freedom and progress, the belief that the exercise of critical reason, beyond all tradition or convention or institution, is the fundamental civic virtue without which other civic virtues cannot be sustained. As educators in pursuit of a secular democracy and a Left-of-Centre polity, we understand and uphold these values of the Enlightenment Left. The radical Right also understands them, but fears them and repudiates them. Thus it is that we dedicate ourselves to the creation of a culture of civility, and they to a culture of cruelty. *That*, ultimately, is at the heart of all our disputes.

The assault on our institutions of education and research is a central element in this project, because these institutions are central in the reproduction of civil society. As Marx once put it:

> In considering such transformations, a distinction must always be made between the material transformation of the

> economic conditions of production, which can be determined with the precision of natural science, and the legal, political, religious, aesthetic, or philosophic – in short, ideological forms in which men become conscious of their conflict and fight it out.

The battle over ideology and consciousness – the battle over all their forms, be they political, or aesthetic, or religious, or philosophic – is thus the central battle, because it is here, in these domains, not simply at the point of production, that human beings actually "fight it out". We of course know that, but they also know it. If they are to re-make India in their own image, they must first win the hearts and minds of our children. It is in this battle that we must engage, because without democratic teachers there shall be no democratic India.

Notes

1 This is the text of a lecture delivered at Delhi University on 11 February 1999 in memory of Ved Gupta, one of the key founders of the Democratic Teachers Front (DTF). The endnotes have been added later.

2 It can be plausibly argued that whereas the other organizations of the Sangh parivar, notably Vishva Hindu Parishad (VHP) and the Bajrang Dal as well as the more recently formed Hindu Jagran Munch (HJM), have used the umbrella of the BJP government, both at the Centre as well as in such states as U. P. and Gujarat, to act on a very broad front ranging from expedited pace of preparation for building the temple at Ayodhya to the attacks on minorities, the cultural project of these governments, at the Centre and in the States, has been focussed on trying to restructure the educational and research institutions, as is indicated in the attempts to revise

textbooks, revamp such institutions as the Indian Council for Historical Research (ICHR), and Hinduise educational practice by introducing the singing of the Vande Mataram and the Sarasvati Vandana in educational institutions. Culture, in the broadest sense, has been a primary target area for the RSS as a whole throughout this period of governmental power.

3 A number of the historians of European fascism, notably Sternhill, have traced the origins of the fascist ideology to the anti-materialist and Romantic critique of Marxism by such figures as Georges Sorel, Charles Maurras and the revolutionary syndicalists toward the end of the 19th century and in the beginning of the 20th century. They have also argued that Mussolini, himself a professed socialist in his early career, was nevertheless deeply inspired by this tradition of hysterical nationalism and the cult of violence, and that he forged what we now know as the classical Italian fascism directly in opposition to the rise of Leninism as the dominant trend in international socialism. See, for instance, Zeev Sternhill (with Mario Sznajder and Maia Asheri), *The Birth of Fascist Ideology: From Cultural Rebellion to Political Revolution*, Princeton University Press, 1994 (original French, 1989). It may be worth mentioning that Ali Shariati, the principal theoretician of the 'left wing' of the Islamic Revolution in Iran, was deeply impressed by the writings of Charles Maurras, just as Moonje was directly inspired by Mussolini himself.

4 The National Front in France and the National Alliance in Italy are only two of the major rightwing groups in Western Europe whose roots in classical fascism of the inter-war years are well known. The Italian variant shall bear a more detailed comment. For forty years, Gianfranco Fini, the leader of this group, happily called himself a fascist or 'neo-fascist'. Then, as his group suddenly emerged as the major coalition partner in the government of Silvio Berlusconi after the Italian elections of 1994, he fleetingly claimed that he was not a fascist but a 'post-fascist' but then, recognizing that the word 'fascist' has fallen into terrible disrepute, he re-named the group as 'National Alliance'. Unlike the fascists of the 1920s and '30s, those of today usually adopt a different name, so as to conceal their true identity. However, their origins in fascist ideology are widely recognized. See, for example, Glynn Ford, *Fascist Europe: The Rise of Racism and Xenophobia*, London, Pluto Press, 1992; or the Special Issue

of *International Socialist* entitled "Euro-Fascism: What makes it Tick?", no. 60, Autumn 1993. Dozens of such analyses are available.

5 This is particularly true of the Croatian leaders and the Serb militias, whose origins date back to the pro-fascist organizations that had fought the civil war against Tito's partisans. However, the political origins of the relatively more benign rulers of Slovenia can also be traced back to those same anti-partisan formations.

6 The origins of India's anti-colonial movement are of course much older but it became a *mass movement* only with the Rowlatt Satyagrah and the Non-Cooperation Movements of the 1919-22 period. Similarly, peasants' and workers' agitations of the modern type had begun already in the 19th century, but the emergence of a mass workers' movement can be traced back – in terms of convenient dates – to the founding of the All India Trade Union Congress in 1920 and the rise of several communist groups as well as Workers' and Peasants' Parties (WPP) over the next few years, reaching a high level of working class militancy during 1927-29 period. RSS arose directly in response – a rightwing obscurantist response – to these developments.

7 Aijaz Ahmad, "Structure and Ideology in Italian Fascism" in *Lineages of the Present*, Delhi, Tulika, 1996.

8 Broadly speaking, we could offer the following schema. 1) The end of the Second World War witnessed an enormous upsurge of anti-colonial movements and a massive wave of decolonisation across Asia and Africa. Great expectations were attached to the rise of the national-bourgeois state as symbolized, for example, in the Bandung Conference and the emergence of the Non-Aligned Movement. 2) The passing of those hopes occurred at different times in different countries, but, on the whole, it was during the ten years between 1965 and 1975 that this type of state reached its crisis, as symbolised, for example, by the defeat of Egypt and Syria in 1967 and the imposition of the Emergency in India some years later. 3) Since the mid-70s – since the 1973 coup in Chile, let us say – there has been little evidence that any national bourgeoisie is seriously interested in defending national independence against imperialist pressures, and the disillusion has become particularly strong over

the past decade. See, for a fuller statement of this position, Aijaz Ahmad, "Introduction: Literature Among the Signs of Our Times", in *In Theory: Classes, Nations, Literatures*, London, Verso, 1992.

9 This critique became particularly influential with the rise to dominance of the anti-communist, postmodern theorists in the wake of the aborted Paris uprisings of 1968. That this dramatic shift in philosophical thinking was led by French intellectuals is not a coincidence. Nor is it a coincidence that this critique, which formalised the dashing of revolutionary hopes, became dominant in the advanced capitalist countries precisely during the years when the newly independent countries of Asia and Africa witnessed the dashing of hopes associated with decolonisation. The early 70s are the years of a triple crisis across the world: the crisis of the national-bourgeois state in the periphery of the capitalist system; the onset of stagnation in the capitalist centres, in the wake of a long wave of prosperity since the late 1940s; and a similar onset of stagnation in the COMECON countries, coupled with their failure to make a transition from extensive industrialisation to intensive industrialisation based on the more up-to-date technologies. This coincidence of various crises is central to the rise of anti-materialist and anti-revolutionary irrationalisms during this period.

10 The characterisation of nationalism as "a derivative discourse" – derived from colonialism itself – is of course the major conceptual contribution of Partha Chatterjee, the most influential of the subalternist theorists, alongside Ranajit Guha. See, in particular, the chapter on Nehru in his *Nationalist Thought and the Colonial World: A Derivative Discourse*, Delhi, Oxford University Press, 1986. The attack on Nehru's emphasis on industrial modernization within a framework of central planning converges, in not altogether agreeable ways, with similar attacks coming from the Right, including the international agencies advocating "liberalisation". Chatterjee seems much perturbed by planning and "modernity" but not much by the market itself. His identification of Gandhi with "tradition" and of Nehru with "modernity" only repeats the conventional wisdom of Indian social science and paves the way for subalternism's later turn toward a full-scale anti-rationalist, indigenist postmodernism.

11 The historic premises of the Indian state as it arose after decolonisation, with its twin emphases on secular democracy and economic

nationalism, were fully under siege by the mid-90s, as the country got overwhelmed by the IMF-inspired "liberalisation" and the RSS-inspired "Hindu nationalism". It was in the midst of this historic shift toward the Far Right that Partha Chatterjee published his well-known essay "Secularism and Toleration" (*Economic and Political Weekly*, XXIX, 28) which questioned the very idea of secularism, a civic virtue enshrined in the Indian Constitution, and affiliated the author explicitly with Ashis Nandy who had by then had a rather extensive red-baiting career. Indeed, Chatterjee was to state that his own essay was a mere continuation of the argument begun by Nandy in his "The Politics of Secularism and the Recovery of Religious Tolerance", in Veena Das (ed.) *Mirrors of Violence: Communities, Riots and Survivors in South Asia*, New Delhi, Oxford University Press, 1992. Subalternism has had a curious career, starting with invocations of Gramsci and finally coming into its own as an accomplice of the anti-communist Right.

Globalization and Culture

I am very grateful to the organizers of this Convention for giving me an opportunity to speak here.[1] I am also glad that Prabhat Patnaik's brilliant and methodical presentation came before mine, which relieves me of the duty to rehearse what little I know about the political economy of imperialism in our time. And, I feel privileged as well as apprehensive about the fact of having Mr. Ashok Mitra in the Chair for this session: privileged because I think of him as something of a sage on the Left, and nervous too on the same count – he surely knows more than me not only about political economy but also about that mysterious thing which we call, for lack of a better word, 'culture'.

That difficulty of speaking about 'culture' in the present climate is compounded for me further by the fact that in this era of imperialist globalization we have witnessed the rise of vast academic complexes and cultural industries which have undertaken to propagate, on the global scale, a singular ideology of what one could accurately call *Culturalism* – an ideology, in other words, which treats culture not only as an integral element in social practices but as the *determining instance*. It is one of the great ironies of ideological production in our time that precisely in the historical moment when capitalism has finally penetrated the farthest reaches not only of economic but also cultural production itself, across the globe, we witness the rise of an ideology, propagated from all the famous pulpits of the Western academy, which shifts the locus of determination from the field of political economy to that of culture.

I shall return to issues of culture presently, at greater length. Let me first detain you, though, in a very condensed and telegraphic way, on how I understand the word 'globalization', since that understanding is what eventually determines, for me, the meaning of 'culture' in our time. I shall not belabour the point that the so-called 'globalization' is the latest phase in the history of imperialism, and that central to it is the sum total of historic shifts in the structure of capital itself. Prabhat clarified all that for us so lucidly this morning. But this is not *simply* a new phase of imperialism but also *radically* a new phase, which could not have come about until after a number of preconditions had been met. What were the most important of those preconditions? I shall answer that question in the form of thirteen inter-linked theses, and what I want to argue is that it is the sum total of all these elements – not some, not this or that – which came to define the radical novelty of this phase.

The first of those preconditions, I believe, was the dissolution of the colonial empires themselves, and the beginning of globalization can thus be dated back to the years following the Second World War. Now, Marx was the first to point out that the drive toward an integrated world market has been inherent in the logic of capitalism from the beginning and that colonialism played the main role in creating such a market. However, between the end of the 15th century, when it all began, until the end of the 18th, the process of real colonization was mostly centred on the Americas and it was only in the 19th century that the interiors of Asia and Africa were intensively colonized, eventually dividing the world into a set of core industrialised countries of the advanced West and a vast hinterland of non-industrialised colonies and dependencies, many of them formally independent. In the days of its final glory, colonialism had created something resembling a world economy but it was a system, really, of interlocking economies, in which different colonial powers controlled different segments. Decolonisation was now necessary for the further development of capitalism as a wholly integrated global economy in this new phase, and the U.S. could not have emerged as an unchallengeable hegemonic power until after its rivals had lost their respective colonial empires.

This then leads to the second precondition, namely that there had to be a pre-eminent power to supervise this transition from a number of large and small empires to a united global empire. The quarter century after the Second World War, which has gone down in history as the golden era of U.S. hegemony corresponds to the organization of that transition. Much has been said more recently about the decline of that hegemony, and it is certainly true that other centres, notably Western Europe and Japan, have also emerged to challenge some aspects of that unique power. It is worth saying, however, that the United States continues to be the most powerful capitalist economy; that the U.S. Federal Reserve still plays the central role in financial markets, of a kind that European and Japanese banks cannot; that the U.S. commands more military power than all of Western Europe and Japan combined; that NATO interventions are really American interventions; that six of the top ten corporations controlling flows of information and cultural goods in the world are American; and that the U.S. has by far the pre-eminent – and I might add, devastating – role in training the techno-scientific-managerial elite of the Third World.

Third, as I just said, the era of classical colonialism had also divided the world into a core of industrialised countries and a vast hinterland of non-industrialised zones. For capitalism to really take off as a universal system, an altogether new kind of division of the world was necessary, between the advanced and the backward capitalist zones. The dissolution of the colonial empires made possible the national bourgeois project of some degree of industrialisation in the Third World and thus vastly altered the very scope of capitalism as such. As the pre-eminent financial, technological and military power of the world, the U.S. was uniquely endowed to shape the whole of this new system in a way no colonial power ever had been. Elsewhere, as in China, that same process of growing industrialisation came to be associated with the non-capitalist path made possible by a combination of domestic revolution and the retreat of semi-colonial imperialism of the type that had been dominant before the revolution; that is the economy that is now being assimilated back into the globalized market fully.

Fourth, the existence of the Soviet bloc and the East Asian socialist and quasi-socialist states had obstructed 'globalization' in three ways. They constituted roughly a third of the world in demographic terms, and that one-third was simply not available for capitalist globalization in the real sense, whatever other relations with the world capitalist market those states might have maintained (witness, for example, the history and mechanics of debt formation among the weaker of the COMECON countries well before the dissolution of the system). Second, they held out the possibility of a challenge to the system of capitalist imperialism as such, on the global scale, as the history of numerous wars of liberation during that period, from Vietnam to Angola and Guinnea-Bissau, would testify. And, third, they served as alternate sources of technology, training, finance and military supplies not only for wars of liberation but also for many of the non-aligned countries, such as Egypt or Syria or India. For us in India, actually, the kind of development we witnessed in key areas of the public sector, from steel to petroleum to petrochemicals, during the first quarter century after independence would have been inconceivable without that alternate source; we managed to avoid the kind of military dependence on the United States that a number of our neighbours, such as Iran and Pakistan, accepted; and, equally crucially, that sense of an alternate pole in international relations helped sustain a certain left-of-centre ideological position for the post-colonial national-bourgeois state. Only with the collapse of the Soviet bloc and the full assimilation of China into the world market could capitalism become a truly global system. All that was accomplished in the last quarter of the 20th century.

The fifth precondition for the full emergence of globalization in its present hegemonic form – namely, the demise of the nationalism of the national bourgeoisie – was also tied up with the demise of that alternate pole, as India's own experience would show; 1989 made no difference to the leading communist force in the country, namely the CPI (M), but did transform the policy positions of the ruling class itself. For roughly a quarter century after the Second World War, economic nationalism in substantial parts of the Third World had presented something of a barrier to truly global triumph of neo-liberalism through a variety of strategies – e.g., protectionism, use of the state sector for growth of domestic industry, relations with the COMECON countries as alternate source for economic aid and technologies – thus somewhat limiting the power of imperialism over their societies. For most of the Third World, that phase began to end in the 1970s and virtually all those countries – Egypt, India, Indonesia, Ghana, Brazil, Guatemala – were assimilated back into the system of dependencies, so that the ones that remained intransigent were now mere islands of local and partial resistance. The final exhaustion of the nationalism of the national bourgeoisie in the Third World coincided then with the dissolution of the Soviet system in Eastern Europe and the USSR as well as the promulgation of the policies of capitalist restoration in China. Only then could a host of Third world regimes begin to act as if there was no alternation to what now came to be called 'globalization'. In India, as you well know, this trend had been evolving for quite some time but it was only by the late 1980s that the national bourgeoisie felt confident enough, thanks to the level of accumulation it had achieved through policies of economic nationalism, to now forego protectionism and integrate itself, as junior partner, with the transnational firms. With the collapse of the Soviet system at the end of that decade even the pretence of non-alignment was dropped.

Sixth, new technologies were required to integrate the world financial markets and make productive capital itself relatively more mobile. This has involved, among other things, the creation of an Information Superhighway, beyond the territorial boundaries of nations and consisting of millions of pathways, whose notable feature is that financial information, commercial messages, entertainment goods and personal correspondence are intermeshed into a single, chaotic flow. The 'virtual' character of much of this flow has been much exaggerated; what one might say, more accurately, is that the kind of global production and exchange which these flows facilitate greatly intensify and extend processes of commodification as well as globalized labour regimes of a historically new kind. In this context, then, neither a world economy nor a world culture, neither global sport nor global entertainment, was possible so long as goods, including financial goods, were exchanged only between individual nations. For globalization of these phenomena, technologies are needed which can beam the same signal into households across the globe and which bring down the travel time for transmission of financial decisions effectively to zero. One might even suggest that the immense technological innovations of the postwar period have been as necessary for the launching of this new, globalized imperialism as the technologies of the Second Industrial Revolution had been necessary for completion of colonial conquest; conversely, globalization of these technologies for production and profit would have been inconceivable without the prior existence of proletariats across the globe on a scale unimaginable in the colonial period.

Seventh, this whole edifice is upheld in a complex system of law and regulation which has two overlapping aspects. There are first of all the regulatory regimes of IMF, the World Bank, the IFIs, GATT, WTO and so on which are, together, fast emerging as a new world government for imposing uniform policies, obligations, and conditionalities around the world, especially the imperialized world. These institutions have been central in perfecting this system, and they of course have their own very complex legal frameworks and regulatory regimes that individual nation-states are to abide by. But an equally crucial aspect of this globalization of law and sovereignty is that national governments are being constantly pressed to alter their own laws so as to make them more compatible with – often mere facsimiles of – American law. The non-territorial empire that has its capital in Washington D.C. thus takes over the actual internal functioning of far-flung nation-states three times over: under the lure and power of private transnational capital, under the regulatory regimes of the supra-national institutions (WTO etc), and by turning the laws of various nations into replicas of American law.

Eighth, this new globalized imperialism also required new types of military technologies, the famous 'automated battlefields' for example, which could deliver imperial power effectively and swiftly against various little enemies that were perceived to be proliferating all over the world, as we have seen in Iraq and the former Yugoslavia, both of which have served as test cases both for military technologies and for moral claims of empire. The deployment of these technologies is then supervised and even executed primarily by the United States, though often in the name of a wider agency; if Iraq was invaded in the name of the UN, war over Kosovo was conducted under the aegis of NATO.

Ninth, just as the supra-national institutions such as the World Bank and WTO are used to impose new imperial regimes of law and regulation, various institutions associated with the UN, most notably the Security Council itself, are increasingly in use for the moral legitimation of imperial aggression. The use of the United Nations to legitimize American military designs is as old as the Korean War of the 1950s. Then, in the period of revolutionary upsurge of the next twenty years, this unholy alliance receded. For a transitory moment in mid-1970s, just about the time of the liberation of Vietnam, the UN had even tried to catch up with the revolutionary temper of the times by enacting a Charter of Economic Rights and Duties of States which proclaimed that member nations had the right not only to "regulate and exercise authority over foreign investment" and "the activities of multinational corporations" but even to "nationalize, expropriate or transfer ownership of foreign property". Thus, in the context of a different balance of global forces, obtained by the revolutionary uprisings and the radical nationalisms of the 1960s, the UN had itself endorsed all the fundamental aspirations of Third World economic nationalism, in ways that would give nightmares to Mr. Kofi Annan who now supervises the re-Americanization of the Security Council. By the time of the military aggression of the Gulf War and the economic aggression of WTO, the Security Council and the UN Secretariat had again been turned into instruments of imperial policy, and Annan's work has been made so very much easier.

Tenth, in addition to the moral legitimation of American aggression by the Security Council, a complex network was required for moral pressure, ideological legitimization and cultural acceptance among the intelligentsias of the world. This was obtained in great many forms, ranging from all kinds of NGOs to high-minded postmodernism to the 'End of History' ideology. It is in this newly emerging moral economy of empire that, as Antonio Negri points out so eloquently, we hear the suave moral philosophers from elite US universities expounding on merits of "just war" – a concept, interestingly enough, first developed in imperial Rome – and the "right of intervention" on the side of human rights etc. That has had a remarkable effect globally, starting with the imperial centres but spreading among the empire's clients in the Third World. If Saddam Hussain was indeed a demon on the issue of human rights then the whole rhetoric of the "Evil Empire" from the days of the Cold War could now be re-mobilized and the death of tens of thousands of Iraqis, from retreating soldiers to hapless children, could then be represented as a regrettable aspect of a just war. It is well to remember, though, that this moral economy also has its own codes and flexibilities. Democracy and human rights are absolute values, except when it comes to places like Saudi Arabia. The drug-dealing and murderous fanatics of Afghanistan get portrayed as moral agents, even 'mujahideen' in the great Islamic cause, so long as they serve as foot soldiers in America's global anti-communist crusade, but they come to personify the worst evils of what came to be called 'Islamic fundamentalism', in high relief, as soon as the communists have been defeated. These cynical flexibilities go largely unnoticed thanks to the prior moral legitimacy created by the Human Rights industry and collusion of the global media.

Eleventh, we are witnessing an evolving new system of sovereignty and citizenship. I have referred already, as have numerous other scholars, to the emergence of new legal regimes. The twin cities of Washington D.C. and New York serve as the combined capital city of this empire because they are the headquarters not only of the U.S. government, which is the decisive fact, but also of most key institutions of this new imperial sovereignty: Wall Street, IMF, the World Bank, WTO, the United Nations and so on. Meanwhile, citizenship is being reorganized in three ways. The collapse of Keynsianism in the core countries and of reformist nationalism in the Third World means that social and economic entitlements are now tied less to citizenship or to employment or to basic survival needs, even in theory, and far more to the market as the final arbiter of the social good; if the market re-distributes incomes upwards, as capitalism would want, instead of downwards, as this People's Convention against Globalization would desire – then so much the worse for the ones at the bottom, who are treated, across the world, the way Kuwait treats its captive, foreign, non-citizen labour. Nor can citizenship survive the death of the nation-state which is routinely, much too hurriedly but jointly announced by high-minded postmodernists and the likes of Madeline Albright, so that nation-states are being re-organized now not as joint projects of common citizenship, or as mechanisms of ensuring the common good of labour humanity within the territorial boundaries of such states, but as differential projects of ethnic identities; Identity today is where Equality once was. Finally, extreme class polarisation produced by the new imperialism on the global scale means that the uppermost stratum commands something like a global citizenship, with few barriers to travel or residence or common consumption patterns and educational facilities – whether the individual member of the stratum lives in Bombay, Delhi, Sao Paulo, Tokyo, Frankfurt, New York, or even Beijing – while the denial of basic entitlements now increasingly envelop considerable numbers of those wretched of the earth who live in those same cities, in their ghettos, barrios, chawls, and of course in the vast rural hinterlands; there are substantial islands of the Third World now in virtually all the major cities of the imperial dominance such as New York, London or Paris. Third World cities are if anything, more brutal. In a city like Shanghai, for example, there are a growing number of peasants – perhaps a couple of hundred thousands in that city already – who have fled from the hinterland but do not have, quite literally, the permission of their state to reside anywhere at all. They live in perpetual hiding and are non-persons in official statistics.

Twelfth, the ideology of globalization has produced much nonsense on the question of the nation-state and its supposed demise in the face of capitalist universalisation. In reality, the nation-state form seems to be alive and proliferating. The United

States has a military establishment that is national – and most jingoistically *nationalist* – to the core. Germany, the most powerful member of the European Union, has just achieved its expanded national consolidation, by virtually colonising the eastern zones. The spectacular growth of the so-called 'East Asian tigers' was unthinkable without the strong interventionist state. Policies of neo-liberal privatisations are carried out across the world by individual nation-states. Capital wants no barriers but labour regimes are always national, even for immigrants as they move from one national regime to another; you only have to ask the Mexicans in Mexico City or, alternatively, in California – not to speak of Indian workers in the Gulf kingdoms. What globalization does want is a nation-state that is *weak* in relation to labour but *strong* on behalf of capital.

Finally, the massive re-organization of Culture. The central fact here is that we are witnessing the emergence of a worldwide capitalist civilization, in which national, regional and local cultures are being re-organized as so many variants of that singular civilization. Civilizational homogeneity exists at the deepest level, the level of commodification. But, at the level of second-order reality – that is to say, in the phenomenal form of the commodity – all kinds of differences are maintained, encouraged, even manufactured – because without that diversification, the illusion of freedom and choice cannot be maintained, which is the very essence of the market. That is why ethnicity is such a major component of modern fashion design, for example, in the global market but also in the national markets that have been re-arranged in the image of the metropolitan markets. Fredrick Engels once wrote optimistically that "every step in the field of culture is a step towards freedom". The poor fellow seems not to have anticipated that the essential cultural project of capitalism was to package every *un*freedom of commodity production in the form of a freedom exercised in the market, by those of course who have money – and the *un*freedom of material life as *freedom* of cultural difference. Walter Benjamin was perhaps closer to the truth when he said that every document of civilization is at the same time a document of barbarism. By 'civilization' of course he meant the capitalist civilization in which acts of aestheticization go hand in hand with acts of monetization, so that use value cannot come to us except as intertwined with its diabolical other – namely exchange value.

With this remark, then, let me take leave of the subject of 'globalization' per se, on which I was not supposed to dilate so extensively, and return to the matter of 'culture' about which some of you mistakenly believe I have some sort of knowledge, if not expertise. I have in fact often wondered what the word 'culture' could possibly mean in the era of this globalization of capitalism, when the farthest corners of agricultural production and subsistence economies are being brought under a single, global law of value, even though the law is enforced differentially in particular nation-states. For, at the deepest level, culture would appear to be, as Samir Amin puts it, that sphere where use values are produced and shared as use values cooperatively and non-coercively, for the satisfaction of needs, which obviously include aesthetic needs, without the mediation of exchange value. Cultural production, in that basic sense, would then appear to be antithetical to commodity production, and the perfection of capitalism would then be equal to a negation of culture as such. This, I believe, is what we mean when we defend the rights, including cultural rights, of the indigenous peoples across the world or the adivasis and the poorest of the peasant communities in India – those, in other words, who are the least integrated into capitalism but the most victimised by it, because their social and cultural forms (even the processes of their material productions) are the least compatible with imperatives of accumulation and patterns of individuation as required by capitalism, especially in its globalized phase when a peculiar combination of national and transnational bourgeoisies, as well as national and transnational bureaucracies, reserve for themselves the right to make critical decisions even about our trees and our waters. In this new era of capitalist universalization, then, the very meaning of the word 'culture' would have to be understood rather differently.

Now, this definition of culture, which I took from Samir Amin and then modified for my own purposes, has a point, even a profound point: the aesthetic pleasure and the purity of the use values of a work of art necessarily diminishes, or at least gets transformed, when it gets caught in circuits of exchange, market pricing, advertising, and so on; and culture itself begins to function as a kind of capital when it is accumulated for the purpose of gaining social distinction and privilege. What needs to be added immediately, however, is that the role of capitalism with respect to culture, in all its phases including the latest phase, is the same as in relation to a great many other things: by improving the means of production it greatly expands the realm of possibility but then its own social relations of production and exchange undermine the very possibilities it opens up. At an earlier stage of development, for example, capitalism created a market for cultural goods and thus freed a substantial number of artists from aristocratic patronage, thus enhancing the potential for an autonomous sphere for art over and above artisanal production, but then it made those same artists captive of that same market, turning every art product that came into its purview into a saleable commodity. In the process, the imperfections of the market also ended up dividing the sphere of art and culture into the local and the national. The local became the sphere where the hold of the market was either non-existent or very restricted, while the national became the sphere where the market sought to dominate. In the more recent phases, right into globalization, then, what happens is that the local too increasingly comes under the domination of the market and the autonomous spheres keep contracting.

Witness, for example, the organization of handicrafts as a government-sponsored sphere in virtually every third world country on the morrow of independence. It was an odd mixture of state sponsorship and petty commodity production, bringing rural authenticity to the urban drawing rooms, which then got increasingly tied to tourism of the individual travellers and then, finally, to globalized export markets. Wittingly or unwittingly, an odd partnership developed in some sphere of NGO activity. Some NGOs aided in organizing the moral economy of empire where issues like Human Rights were used not only to de-legitimize the nation-state, which was cruel and illegitimate enough, but also to appoint multi-national agencies and even imperial states as the guardians of those human rights. In a parallel move, a quasi-aesthetic, quasi-cultural sphere of petty production was organized where some of the most oppressed sections of society – peasant and tribal women, for instance – were mobilized to produce for elite consumption, nationally and internationally. Here, I am not raising the issue of intentions, because intentions were very frequently admirable; it was all done in pursuit of what got called "empowerment" – empowerment of *women* most frequently. I am much more interested here in the power of the market to subsume projects of this kind for its own expansion and to use perfectly well-intentioned people as its moral agents and cultural representatives. And, I am interested in the contradictory structure of the Real itself, in which those projects of empowerment which work within the market economy often turn out to be the other face of globalization.

For a Marxist, in any case, there is really no escape from trying to ponder that vision of culture which thinks of it as a sphere where use values are produced non-coercively and shared without the mediation of exchange-value, for the satisfaction of common needs, including aesthetic needs. At a lower level of theoretical abstraction, though, one could also address the issue of culture through other definitions, which are essentially humanistic and sociological. Three such definitions interest me: culture as a zone of the aesthetic and the intellectual; culture as a 'whole way of life'; and, in a more materialist emphasis, culture as the sum of those means and practices of communication through which meanings and values are produced and disseminated.

Of these three, the definition of culture as a 'whole way of life' is perhaps the more common, commanding the widest agreement; and it is from this conception that ideas of a 'national culture', an 'Indian culture', a 'Hindu culture', a 'Western culture' and so on, are derived. Now, to my mind, a society which is fundamentally divided along lines of power and powerlessness, be they class powers or power of men over women, or the power structures within a community of religious belief – a society that is riven with oppositions so fundamental could hardly share a singular culture. Culture, in such instances, functions not as an unfolding of the National Spirit but as a field of struggle and contention. The same applies to communities of belief which usually get represented in the dominant discourses as unified entities. Not only is it impossible for a caste society to have a unified culture, even the very history of Brahminism and the many dissents which arose against it, including theistic dissents, would tend to disabuse us of the idea of a singular, transcendent religious culture. It seems to me facile and erroneous to identify culture with nation or religion. What we find in all such cases is not a unified culture, not a unity-in-diversity as the benign phrase goes, but a variety of cultures in mutual combat. Nor is culture a static, trans-historical category, as most aestheticised notions of cultures tend to romanticise it. In the modern world, at least, what does not change in cultural practices is the principle and process of change itself. Finally, culture is not always a zone of freedom, self-expression, self-realization, community-sharing etc. Culture, including traditional culture, is just as frequently a zone of Un-freedom and entrapment, as any number of oppressed members of specific communities can tell you.

I wanted to go through some of these negative definitions simply to say what is so obvious: that, the real question always is: Whose culture? And the question with respect to globalization is: whose culture, within the nation, does it destroy the most thoroughly, and whose culture does it support ideologically and strengthen materially, through all sorts of means including the electronic means, the means of telecommunication and digitization, concentrations of investible capital, etc., which it makes available to some cultural practices and denies to some other. When I oppose the cultural intervention of globalized capital in India, I don't want to fall in the trap of a conventional kind of nationalistic jingoism. I don't oppose the culture of globalization in the name of an Indian, a Hindu, a Muslim, a Third World culture, and so on. My own opposition is much more fundamental. The culture of globalization destroys within India certain ways of life and sustains some others; it puts the most advanced means of cultural combat in the hands of some and denies them to others;

it intervenes, savagely, in a cultural struggle that is peculiarly our own; it seeks to pre-empt the possibility that we shall settle these issues in our way, among contenders within the nation. That is where I entirely depart from a kind of nationalism that I take to be a reactionary, indigenist notion of the defence of national culture, because that kind of defensiveness presumes that what is to be defended is a national culture that already exists. What one wants to defend, rather, are the cultures of the victims of globalization but not the cultures of its beneficiaries. And one wants to defend, in the teeth of globalization, the *right* to make one's nation, hence one's own national culture, according to the needs and requirements of our own people. National culture, in this definition, is not something inherited or already achieved; it is a horizon yet to be met, and a horizon that will keep receding so long as we have not, collectively, met the most fundamental of democratic demands for social change – in the insurrectionary sense of that phrase, 'democratic demand'. And, it is in this most fundamental sense that globalization is a pre-emptive counter-revolution that seeks to make itself permanent.

Let me then return to the more modest, more materialist definition of culture as the sum of means and practices through which values and meanings are generated. I like this definition because the idea of the *generation* of meaning gives to the idea of 'culture' an orientation not toward the past but toward the future; the dimension not only of inheriting but also of making, and the idea of a common possession over which the various forces within a society contend. The definition of it as the sum of means and practices gives to culture a materiality of its own, beyond all mysticism inherent in phrases like 'structures of feeling'; culture is what one *does*. And if culture is a contradictory totality of a sum of practices by contending parties, then there shall undoubtedly be cultural practices compromised deeply by violence and domination, but also, always, other moments which would be moments of insurgent cultural practice that shall go on imagining the impossible and thus keep its promise to the future.

This orientation toward the future, this will and capacity to go on imagining the impossible, is what the culture of globalization seeks to fatally undermine. How so? What are some of the more notable aspects of that other kind of culture, which also generates values and meaning? I have already spoken of some of its basic features. Let me emphasize some others, as quickly as possible, and, because I am speaking in front of a select audience I will skip details of monopoly etc.

There is, first, the invasive reach. To comprehend the reach, we only have to recall the colonial classroom which reached a very small cross-section of the nation's children. The ideology of colonialism was dispensed much more obliquely, from behind the textbooks as it were. Children spent relatively few hours and days in those classrooms and then returned to homes that were ideologically rather detached from the classroom. Perhaps not much more than ten per cent of the populace in India went through the exercise; the rest were subjected to it indirectly and imperfectly. The culture of globalization, by contrast, comes not only through the classroom which now includes a much larger proportion of the population but also, more centrally, certainly for the middle classes, within the household through such instruments as television and commercialised music, on a daily basis. The intensity of this invasion of the household itself then changes not only thought processes but also the lived value systems, consumption patterns, and even the very nature of such human desires as love and sexuality. It is at least arguable that even as literacy in the conventional sense has spread more than during the colonial period, electronic literacy is even much more widespread in today's India, and much more active in transforming the lived culture, than the ordinary literacy in reading and writing could be. The direct influence of these processes is of course greatest among the affluent classes, but those are also the decisive classes in shaping the cultures of the classes they dominate. Nor is there some great Wall of China insulating the working people from the mediatized lives of the rich; indeed, electronically manipulated culture has a wide reach even among those who do not possess the gadgets, since, for example, groups of poor families routinely rent TVs and VCRs to participate in that culture as passive, fantasizing consumers.

Then there is the globalization of cultural form. Institutions of mass culture and popular entertainment, which have a much deeper reach into the working class neighbourhoods and countryside than ever before, are also much more closely integrated into the dominant American media ideologically, politically, aesthetically and in expressive form; not to speak of the fact that with the onset of neo-liberalism, foreign media itself dominates the TV channels, even in India where this was unimaginable barely a decade ago. Every session of TV watching, to which the whole of the Indian middle class is addicted, turns out to be a study circle for acquisition of certain sorts of ideology and cultural taste; and re-making oneself in the image of the American teenager becomes a widespread form of imagined class mobility among those whose positions at the bottom of the class ladder may remain stationary in material terms. This globalization of cultural form and patterns of deep desire is achieved notably through advertising, logo promotions and interconnections between all that and entertainment itself, where iconic figures of the culture industry get to be identified closely with particular products and product signs. Sachin Tendulkar and Shahrukh Khan become interchangeable icons of mass culture in the selling of Pepsi. In the process, Sachin, the legendary batsman, himself becomes an entertainer and a salesman like any other – very much in the image of Michael Jordan, the hero of American basketball and a central figure in the selling of sports as commodity and entertainment. This, then, is to be connected with globalization of certain advertising images. While trying to get to the channel that would give me cricket in the Eden Gardens yesterday I came upon a cascading river of black hair, a different sort of Eden as it were, and assumed that it was the familiar ad for the shampoo 'Heads and Shoulders' that I have seen numerous times on Indian TV, only to find that I was actually watching the ad for that same shampoo on Pakistani TV, where the visual image of shining black hair was exactly the same but now came with a different voice, face and spoken text. Part of the objective of this crusading cultural globalizm is the creation of new tastes by associating them with patterns of American life and thus giving to the Indian middle classes the sense of having arrived at a global cultural scene. Witness, for example, the sports channels that relentlessly show things like golf and baseball which have had no presence in India before the advent of cable television just a few years ago; the aim seems to be to *make* an audience for these heretofore foreign sports. At this intersection of commerce and entertainment which passes for culture, though, the main maneauver of globalized electronic cultural form is that it seeks to transform elite culture as well as mass culture in a single sweep. The colonial cultural project was deeply tied to the aspirations of the upper layers of the Indian propertied classes, as they wished to move closer to the image of the Oxbridge Englishman of their dreams and farther away from the rest of Indian society; Anglicizing colonial culture was thus deeply tied to *increasing* the cultural gap between the rich and the poor within Indian society. The cultural project of globalizing capitalism, on the other hand, has a curious levelling effect where the United States is itself undergoing increased Disneyfication, which is then exported to all classes in the advanced as well as backward capitalist zones, for the edification of all classes that have access to television or are under the influence of those who have that access.

Counterpoised against this reach is the concentration of privilege in other areas of globalizing technologies, especially the cutting edge technologies, namely the Internet and the World Wide Web, which are very much worth considering since we hear so much these days of the democratizing effects of IT which is said to make information widely available across the globe. As Bill Gates immortally put it: "All are equal in *virtual* reality." Well, in real reality, however, half of living humanity has never made a phone call and there are more telephone lines in the Manhattan Island of New York than there are in the whole of Africa. How do you then travel from the really real to the virtually real? Some 70 percent of the world's income is produced and consumed by 15 per cent of the world's population which then fairly well represents the access to information goods. North America and Northwestern Europe together account for less than 20 per cent of the world's population but some 70 per cent of the world's income, and it is no surprise, therefore, that they also own two-thirds of the world's TV and radio sets.

Even within the advanced industrial countries, ownership of any considerable Internet access has been a relative class privilege. Start-up costs would have to cover increasingly more sophisticated and powerful equipment, costing at least $2000, which is then regularly replaced or at least substantially upgraded every few years. No wonder that surveys indicate a relative correlation between regular use of the Internet and high incomes: a third of the users in Britain have an annual income of 25,000 pounds while a third in the U.S. and Canada make upward of $80,000.

It may well be said that the Internet is less than a decade old and has already spread so very much; in another two decades it will probably reach the remotest corner of the earth; the Internet Cafe would seem to be the instrument universalising this access. That the Internet will spread enormously in the long as well as the short term seems to me obvious, but that everyone, or even a majority of people, will get wired in any foreseeable future seems to me not so obvious. The first telegraph lines were laid in the 1830s and a telegraph line between London and Bombay was completed by 1865; in the West universally, and among the urban middle classes of the industrialised zones in the Third World, a telephone line is now simply taken for granted, but much of humanity has not yet received a telegram and, as I just said, half of humanity is still waiting to make a phone call.

It is unlikely that the Internet shall be anything but a minoritarian and privileged cultural instrument in the foreseeable future. The expert culture – those who have the personal or institutional means to use it – will benefit enormously. Research and the communication of the fruits of research will be faster and more comprehensive, and the ease of communication shall bring, at any given moment, a much larger community of experts into direct communication. This community of experts itself is likely to experience this whole process as greater democratization of information and access. In reality, expert culture shall be consolidated and expanded far beyond anything print technology ever could have achieved, but the distance between the expert and non-expert cultures will also have increased greatly, at least for the foreseeable future. The world is fast getting divided between those who can send and receive e-mails regularly, and those who cannot; a more extended use of the Net narrows the number of the privileged further. Indeed, if you have the Net, you can be in much more intimate and regular contact with someone living in Chicago than with someone else who lives at the other end of Delhi but does not have a phone.

What I want to emphasize is the contradictory effect of every new technology. For, every new technology in the field of culture and communication has a liberating potential; it can shorten the time of labour and rationalize the process of labour; it can widen the community of cultural communication and bring more people within the circuit of modern cultural production; it can open up new arenas of experiment and innovation. That is why one must never fall into the anti-modernist trap and start opposing the technology itself. What one must constantly oppose, rather, is the social relations of production and possession which turn every potential for liberation into an instrument of domination.

I have so far concentrated on the key means of communication that have come to India in the age of globalization. But the main thing about culture is that it exists in all aspects of life and is simply inseparable from zones of the economic, political, military and so on. As neo-liberalism came to India, we have seen rapid degradation of political culture as a whole. Hardly any newspaper is now left, at least among the national dailies in the English language, which gives greater priority to news than to advertisement; *Times of India*, was still a serious newspaper as late as the 1980s but then increasingly became a semi-pornographic broadsheet which uses bits of news to fill up the spaces between advertisements. This then is connected with that other kind of pornography – the pornography of power. As masses of people in Iraq were mercilessly wiped out through the most barbaric means of imperial aggression, Indian newspapers were admiringly reporting the great technological wonders hidden in the latest of the American weapons deployed in that 'automated battlefield'. At the same time, these same newspapers have re-modelled themselves on the model of mass-circulation American dailies which specialise in trivia; if the front pages get occupied by an Indian beauty queen one day, divorce of an American movie star makes front page news the next day.

There are many such issues, but we hardly have the time to address them all. In closing, though, let me say that the culture of globalization is not simply an external imposition but also arises, spontaneously as it were, from the life process of the affluent classes within India. That is why it ought not be treated in the terminology of invasion and defence. It is useful to recall that much of what is progressive and valuable in modern Indian society and culture came initially from Europe; Marxism and communism, liberal democracy, secularism, trade unions, printing technologies, a free press, modern civil and criminal codes and an independent judiciary – all these originated in Europe and we have used them for our own purposes, as we also use the railways and factory-made goods. The worst aspect of the integration of India into capitalist universality is that it is bringing to us not the best but the worst of western civilizational and cultural values; in the best parts of the cultures of the advanced capitalist west there is actually much that we need to appropriate for our own purposes. Meanwhile, the ones who periodically stage demagogic protests against the so-called 'western invasion' – I mean, the Shiv Sainiks, the Swadeshi Jagran Manch, and so on – are also the political agents of parties and governments most deeply committed to opening up the Indian markets for western finance and re-writing Indian laws to suit American investors. Indeed, they cannot go beyond mere symbolic gestures because not only their government but also their main social base – in the upper-class, upper-caste, big-city mercantile bourgeoisies and saffron yuppies – is comprised of the greatest enthusiasts of liberalization.

As we look back at the past fifty years of our history, we actually find a very significant contrast. Those sections of the national bourgeoisie who pursued, in the early decades of the Republic, the ideologies of secularism, modernity and 'socialistic and planned development' of the national economy, were also the ones who were committed to a non-aligned and independent foreign policy and, at home, a kind of cultural anti-imperialism. By contrast, those propagandists of the Far Right who claim now to speak for cultural nationalism, the true Indian religion and tradition, etc., are also the ones who have made the most extensive and rapid surrender to imperialist capital. This gives to communalism itself a very peculiar kind of aggressivity. I have argued elsewhere that in a country like India which has massive traditions of anti-colonial nationalism in its past and which is presently the object of imperialist domination, a nationalist ideology is an objective necessity, and if the progressive forces are unable to lead this nationalist current into anti-imperialist directions a retrograde and reactionary force will surely try to full that vacuum. Today, the RSS and its friends want to spread a communalised version of cultural nationalism because they dare not practice anti-imperialist nationalism. Symbolic battles are fought in the hope that the people shall thus be induced to forget the real battles. Since they cannot and will not defy the United States or the World Trade Organization (WTO), which are the real oppressors, they will stage a symbolic protest against outlets of Kentucky Fried Chicken. Having surrendered to imperialism, however, they dare not persist in the symbolic battle either, since any real attack on any arm of the U.S. corporate capital might scare away other corporate investors as well. That is why even "foreign invasion" is constantly re-defined in irrationalist and culturalist terms. What threatens India, it is now said, is not the imperialist invasion of today but the so-called 'Muslim' invasion of medieval times, not foreign corporate capital but "foreign religions", notably Islam and Christianity, so that the destruction of mosques and churches – the very living symbols of these "foreign" religions – is presented as acts of redemption of the national honour precisely at the time when the nation's publicly owned assets are being sold to foreign investors and domestic capitalists alike, for a song. In short, then, the Hindu Jagran Manch is so aggressive, deflecting attention from the real problems of anti-imperialist nationalism, because the Swadeshi Jagran Manch is a fakery through and through, incapable of protecting any of the nation's real assets.

Note

1 This paper includes passages from my article "Globalization: A society of Aliens?", *Frontline*, October 13, 2000, and from the Safdar Hashmi Memorial Lecture I delivered in November last year. Some phrases and ideas have been taken from Samir Amin, Antonio Negri, Susan George and others.